TABLE TALK

TABLE TALK

▼ Easy Activity and Recipe Ideas for ▼
Bringing Your Family Closer at Mealtime

Mimi Wilson & Mary Beth Lagerborg

FOCUS ON THE FAMILY

PUBLISHING
Colorado Springs, Colorado

Table Talk
Copyright © 1994 by Mimi Wilson and Mary Beth Lagerborg. All rights reserved.
International copyright secured.

Wilson, Mimi
        Table talk / by Mimi Wilson and Mary Beth Lagerborg.
                p. cm.
        Includes index.
        ISBN 1-56179-254-3
        1. Communication in the family. 2. Family. 3. Dinners and dining.
4. Table-talk.   I. Lagerborg, Mary Beth. II. Title.
    HQ734.W759   1994
    306.87—dc 20   94-14105
                                                       CIP
Published by Focus on the Family Publishing, Colorado Springs, Colorado 80995.
Distributed by Word Books, Dallas, Texas.

Editor: Ken Durham
Designer: Product Concept Consulting, Inc.
Cover Illustration: Marian Hirsch

Printed in the United States of America

94 95 96 97 98 99/10 9 8 7 6 5 4 3 2 1

▾ Dedication ▾

With love to
Ella Deans Spees and Elisabeth Carruth Chubb,
our mothers.

▾ Contents ▾

▾ Acknowledgments ▾

Table Talk includes table tidbits from many friends and relatives, including recipes, family experiences, and help with research and editing. We're thankful for their contributions and for the ways they have enriched our lives:

Barbara Andrews	Lynette McKinney
Cynthia Bahlman	Mardell Peterson
Ann Benson	Becky Simms
Delores Buttram	Shannon Sperte
Margaret Garcia	Shelly Volkerhart
Anne Gates	Becky Wilson
Karen Johnson	Dawn Wilson
Jo Kadlecek	Debbie Wilson
Nanci Keatley	Don and Chris Wilson
Melissa Masoner	Julie Witt

We couldn't have completed this venture without the support of our husbands, Calvin Wilson and Alex Lagerborg, who have encouraged all the work and travel across two continents required for us to pull this book together. We also are grateful for their smiling faces at the heads of our family tables.

2

▾ Introduction ▾

In 1982, Mimi Wilson and I wrote *Once-a-Month Cooking*. Actually what we wrote was its predecessor, a spiral-bound booklet titled *Freeze and Save*. (Mimi's husband called it "Thaw and Chaw.") We hadn't intended to write it; we did it to help Mimi save time.

Both of us were in the blessed backwaters of raising three children at home. Mimi performed time studies on how she spent her days, which included marketing handcrafts of Laotian refugees, doing some church work, and entertaining lots of company. Her husband, Cal, was a family physician, so his schedule was intense. Mimi realized she wasted a great deal of time fixing the evening meal from scratch each day. Determined to cut her cooking time, yet wanting to maintain the quality of her meals and have plenty on hand for company, Mimi assembled an entire week's dinner entrées and froze them. As she got the hang of it, she began assembling two weeks' dinner entrées at once. Finally, one cooking day when she finished there were 30 entrées on the counter.

As word spread among Mimi's friends, they wanted to know how to do it, too. So one day, Mimi called me. (In our spare time she and I had been writing articles together like "Nursing Sick Children at Home" and "Creating the Trip of a Lifetime for Your Children." We used Mimi's experiences, and I wrote. The royalties, which we split, totaled $100 for a couple of years' work.)

"Beth," she said, "why don't you call the *Denver Post* and see if they would like us to do an article on my method of cooking?" I was petrified.

"Mimi, *you* call the *Post* and let me know what they say," I replied. What they told her was that they would send a reporter and photographer to her house within a week to do a Wednesday food feature. Sure enough, the next week the *Post* featured a story along with a picture of Mimi and her five-year-old son, Kevin. Our lives would never be the same.

For the next several weeks Mimi's telephone rang constantly. People who had read the article wanted her to explain how to do it. The only problem was that Mimi's objective had been to save time; now she couldn't get away from the phone.

A year later, when another local paper wanted to run an article on the method, Mimi called me again. "Look," she said. "let's put the method in a booklet. Then we can use the article to advertise that it's available through the mail." Thus *Freeze and Save* was born. I typed the recipes, shopping lists, and the steps involved in assembling the entrées; then our children helped us collate and bind the book.

Three days after the article ran I opened my mailbox and found it stuffed with 63 envelopes—and that was only the beginning.

In the following months we formed a business partnership with a fill-in-the-blanks incorporation form we found at the library. So that no one could steal our idea, we also filled out a generic copyright form and sent it to the Library of Congress along with the requisite $10 and two copies of our book. The clerk who filed our books called to order a copy.

A few months later, a local video production company asked to videotape Mimi demonstrating the method. They asked us to expand the book and told us they would produce and market both products. Since we didn't understand the contract they submitted to us, we hired an attorney, a family friend. Our primary goal at that point was not to get involved in something our husbands would have to bail us out of. They were being supportive—although perhaps not taking us seriously—and we didn't want to blow it.

The morning of our appointment with the attorney, I called Mimi. "What are you wearing?" I asked. We had to nail down that detail wherever we went. We happened to have identical skirts and were afraid we'd show up looking like the Bobbsey Twins. By the time I left that day, I felt exceptionally well put together in a new dress with matching shoes and purse.

Our attorney showed us into a mohagany-furnished boardroom. The Denver skyline loomed over us through a huge plateglass window. We felt terribly important. After an initial conversation, he asked us into his office. When I reached down to get my purse, I discovered the shoulder strap was wound around the caster on the leg of my chair. As I stooped to lift the chair leg and untangle my purse strap, the attorney looked back at me from the doorway. I no longer felt so well put together.

The videotaping was not too glamorous either. The camera crew set up their gear in my kitchen at 8:30 Monday morning. It was early July, and like most Denver homes, ours had no air conditioning. It's really only needed one week of the summer, but that happened to be the one week of the summer we needed it.

The video crew closed the windows and covered them with an amber film. By 10:00 A.M. the camera was ready. Mimi was positioned at the counter in a green-and-white striped dress and a kelly green apron with MIMI embroidered on it. She would say a few lines, then *cut/repeat* them, *cut/repeat* them, *cut*, say a few more, *cut/repeat* those, *cut*, and so on.

As we inched our way through the day, Mimi's outfit grew limp, and the food became rancid. Mimi read cue cards, perspired, and lost weight. Meanwhile, I held cue cards and ate. (I gained five pounds that week.) By the time the crew left at 11:00 P.M., Mimi was so spent she was stammering and dropping measuring cups. Rotting casserole dishes covered the kitchen counter, their odors trapped with us in the room. And that was just the first day with four more to go.

I had placed my children with a sitter all week to get them out of the house, and by Friday my oldest, seven-year-old Tim, was hanging onto the car door handle and crying as I drove away.

Seven months later, we met with the video company. They told us they were truly sorry, but they didn't have the money to complete our project. They gave us the edited master videotape and the typeset, revised manuscript. For the next six weeks we were in grief, or at least shock. We owed money to our attorney. Would our husbands have to bail us out after all?

No. We finally pulled ourselves together and went to a bank to apply for a line of credit. We would pay our debt, publish the book, and then market the book and videotape to repay the loan. The banker peered at us from behind his tortoise-shell glasses. "Ladies," he asked, "what do you have to offer as collateral?" We looked at each other and shrugged.

"Six kids?" Mimi replied.

Somehow, we got the loan.

The book, renamed *Dinner's Ready: The Once-a-Month Cooking Method*, got some good breaks which, in light of our naivete in marketing, we recognize as divine intervention. It was reviewed in a newsletter published by the Side-Tracked

Home Executives, which resulted in mail orders from around the country. It also was reviewed by Bonnie McCullough, a home-management specialist, in her *Denver Post* column. Soon after that review we returned home from the mountains one Sunday evening to find *Dinner's Ready* listed in the *Denver Post's* local best-seller list. That night I ran from house to house through my neighborhood collecting more copies of the list.

Then Bonnie McCullough called again. "I forgot to tell you," she said, "my column also appears in the *LA Times* and the *Dallas Morning News* and the. . . . " It was a heady time for us—but of course it didn't last forever. And since our business was nearly all mail-order, it was a lot of hard work.

One summer Mimi took her cooking method abroad. She, her husband Cal, and the children took a short-term mission trip to Peru. Word came to Cal, who was working at a jungle hospital, that a tribe that had never contacted the outside world was dying of an unknown illness. Two of the tribe's men had recently visited a downriver village, and when they returned they unknowingly carried a disease against which the tribe had no immunity.

Cal, a translator, and a nurse hiked into the jungle where they found the entire tribe prone in their hammocks. Some were already dead; all the others were gravely ill. Limited to what they could carry on their backs, the team had brought in only medicine, a shortwave radio, and a minimum amount of food.

Cal and his team immediately injected all the survivors with penicillin. Then he contacted Wycliffe mission headquarters by radio and asked the missionaries to have Mimi send food via a JAARS airplane drop. Mimi prepared freeze-and-save cuisine, packaged it in airtight containers, wrapped each parcel in newspaper, and took it all to the airstrip. The next day it was airlifted to the stricken village. The frozen food survived the drop in good shape, Cal and the team were sustained, and the Indians were saved.

Both Cal and Mimi had a heart for missions, and after their experience in Peru and an earlier short-term stint at a Zaire hospital, they knew it was only a matter of time before they would go to the mission field to stay. That time came in 1986, and the Wilsons prepared to move to Quito, Ecuador.

At that point, we knew we needed a publisher to take on the task of producing and marketing *Dinner's Ready*. St. Martin's Press accepted the project and published the book. The title was changed again, this time to *Once-a-Month Cooking*.

A few days before the Wilsons' big move—a third of their belongings stored, a third sold, a third packed to go with them—they invited our family over for breakfast. (I've always marveled at the way Mimi graciously invites company into their home no matter what else is going on.) As the 10 of us ate in the breakfast room, the movers were busy hauling the dining room table out the front door.

In Quito, God provided Mimi the gift of a househelper named Rosa. Rosa spoke no English, so she helped Mimi learn Spanish. She also loved to cook and was able to adapt the once-a-month method to Ecuadorian foods. Rosa had a heart for hospitality to rival Mimi's, and before long Mimi was teaching cooking classes, with Rosa's help, to Ecuadorian women.

Mimi and I now see each other for a few days a year at best, when the Wilsons come to Denver on furlough. Two phrases characterize our long distance partnership. One is Mimi's "tell me every juicy detail"—meaning book details—

when we talk in person or on the phone. The other is her question, "Do you want payment in leather?" When Mimi sells cookbooks in Ecuador, instead of converting my half of the Ecuadorian *sucres* to dollars, she sends me leather hand luggage which she can purchase very inexpensively in rural markets.

The final chapter of our cookbook saga unfurled in the spring of 1990. A guest of Dr. James Dobson's on a Focus on the Family radio broadcast mentioned how much she had been helped and how much money she had saved using *Once-a-Month Cooking*. That May I received a call from Focus on the Family telling me they were considering airing a broadcast on the cooking method. They asked if Mimi and I could come to Pomona, California, to tape the broadcast in July. It just so happened Mimi was coming to the U.S. in July and had planned to fly to California to visit her mother.

We traveled together, met Dr. Dobson and Mike Trout—who were both warm and genuine—and taped the broadcast. We were amazed that Dr. Dobson knew exactly what to ask each one of us. And the session seemed to go so quickly that we couldn't even remember what we had said until the broadcast aired.

The clincher came when Focus on the Family told us they wanted to publish the book. We were astounded. The Focus on the Family version, expanded to include a two-week cycle of low-fat entrées, was published in April 1992.

After the adventures we've had, we never cease to be grateful for the number of people who tell us the method has met their specific family needs of saving time in the kitchen, saving money, and consistently providing a nutritious evening meal. We cannot imagine the scope of needs the method has met as it has subsequently been featured in *Focus on the Family* magazine and *The National Enquirer*.

Many times Mimi and I have been asked if we will write another installment of *Once-a-Month Cooking*. We try to explain that Mimi devised the method and that we originally wrote the book so we could spend *less* time in the kitchen and get on with our lives. In Mimi's case, that means caring and obtaining treatment for disabled children in Ecuador, where she has been asked by the Ecuadorian government to set up a group home for disabled youth. She constantly entertains company, along with hosting Bible studies and keeping up with Cal's medical work. For my part, I've gone on to other writing projects.

However, we did want to give voice to the passion we feel for making home a haven and making mealtime a respite—a time for the family to connect with one another in our fast-paced, fragmented world. As our own families grow up and leave home, we'll miss those times as we look forward to our grandchildren's smiling faces and little hands at our tables.

Alive through these pages are family experiences and creative ideas from a host of wonderful friends. We thank them all, especially Kirk and Dawn Wilson, who provide a stateside home for Mimi's family when they visit. We hope the ideas we share will strengthen the bonds within your family and provide rich memories to sustain each person around your table.

▼ CHAPTER 1 ▼

CALLED TO THE TABLE

The family table provides an
oasis in a helter-skelter world.

I f I had to choose one piece of furniture to keep through the years until Alex and I move to Greener Pastures Nursing Home, it would be our breakfast table. My parents bought it for us years ago when they came to visit and discovered that we newlyweds ate at a card table. When we picked it out, we somehow had the sense to choose a sturdy round, wooden model with two extra leaves and six chairs. It has served us well.

After 20 years of wear, the worn places on the seats and scuff marks on the rungs speak of use and of life. The table, marred by model glue and a pumpkin carving knife, is haunted with memories of a host of friends and of our children from high chairs to high school. It represents the best of what we've had and of what we will have together as a family and as a team.

Americans sense the significance of gathering the family for dinner. Miss Manners, a columnist on etiquette, calls dinner "the cornerstone of family life and, indeed, civilization itself."[1] In fact, in a *Los Angeles Times* survey, 86 percent of those polled said they consider eating dinner with their families to be "very important." The respondents viewed dinner as "the linchpin for the day, a respite from the chaos and separation in daily life."[2]

Most families realize the need to spend regular, focused time together in order to tune in to one another, to develop a sense of identity, and to enjoyably open their home to guests. Yet actually circling the wagons, gathering the family, and preparing the meal—aye, there's the rub!

Mealtime is assaulted from all sides: work schedules, sports practices, music lessons, and fitness classes. It often is undercut by poor meal planning. Television and the telephone add to the opposition. Too often, any attempt at a calm, sane family mealtime succumbs to the competition.

As Americans we spend fewer hours working or sleeping than we did 20 years ago. Yet we feel much more harried because society persuades us there are more things we *must* do. As a result, a consistent family gathering time suffers.

For some families, it's just not possible to be together for dinner, and they must be more creative to accomplish time together. One single mom liked to relax with a cup of tea and cookies late in the evening. Soon, her two children began joining her on different nights. After a while they found the time together so cozy that now the three of them regularly share "tea at ten."

Another family in which the father manages a restaurant at night has designated breakfast as family time. At 7:00 o'clock every weekday morning they meet at the table for a simple breakfast followed by Bible reading and singing. On Sunday morning the menu and the table setting are more elaborate, and the grandparents are their guests.

But whether our gathering time is at breakfast, midday meal, dinner, or 10:00 P.M., the same questions apply. How can we capture that focused time more regularly? How can we make the most of that time? And how can we eliminate complaints and quarrels and instead fill the time with laughter and open communication? Answering these questions is the heart of *Table Talk*.

Some families have wrestled with mealtime and have won. As one working mom with a blended family says, "Dinner is our best time. We savor every minute. It's the only time except weekends we can count on being together, even though it's only every other week. The kids really let their hair down. Everyone gets a chance to talk. Dad controls the teasing and put-downs, and ensures that everyone has equal time. There's always candlelight, and we take turns choosing dinner music."

For these kinds of families we've offered topics for table conversation, menu ideas, and ways to open the home to share with company the great thing they've got going.

On the other hand, your family—like many in our world today—may be facing an entirely different situation. Barb, a mother of two, said she and her husband used to pick up the children from childcare after work and grab dinner along a fast-food strip on the way home. One evening Barb finally overdosed on this routine and prepared dinner at home.

"Mommy, I want a meal," her young daughter complained.

"But, Honey, this is a meal," she replied, exasperated.

Finally it occurred to Barb that her daughter equated dinner with a Happy Meal. So she attempted to cook dinner more often, though it wasn't easy. Used to making their own menu selections, her family members were difficult to please.

Of course, dinner doesn't have to be at home all the time. Americans increasingly eat out or drive through. Take-out Chinese and order-out pizza have their place. The real issue is the *quality* of time a family experiences eating at home or away. Are we maintaining good time together?

If we abandon our consistent family mealtime, we lose a forum in which family members can express their crazy ideas, their dreams, their frustrations, their fears, and their pleasures. We lose a sounding board for opinions about presidential candidates and ideas for a great family vacation. We lose the base from which most family traditions are built, and our children lose a chance to grow in self-esteem and life skills and to learn good manners in a nonthreatening setting.

We may also lose the opportunity to bring a bit of happiness to a person or family who needs acceptance and a warm meal. Gone is the chance to expand our world view by having guests who are different from ourselves in nationality, race, or religion. We may lose a natural training ground for children, a place where parents talk and children learn about values, cultural preferences, current events, and how their parents see God moving in the world.

Larry and Shirley Rascher were missionaries in Irian Jaya, New Guinea, when their children were young. Their family of seven would gather for dinner by lantern light, with strips of masking tape hung above the table to trap hovering insects. Through the window screens, nationals would watch and listen silently as the *tuans,* or white people, took their meal together. The Raschers would tell stories and laugh long into the tropical night. The older children attended a boarding school on the island, so when they were all together during school vacations they had a lot to tell. And with such rich family times to sustain them, the children could leave for weeks at boarding school with their emotional tanks filled and their hearts refreshed.

What does a family gain that regularly breaks bread together? If care is taken to keep conversation positive, a family enjoys a huge boost toward general good health and a sense of belonging. Dolores Curran, family specialist and author of *Traits of a Healthy Family*, found that a healthy family values its table times and mealtime conversations.[3]

One big advantage, says a mother of grown children who enjoyed regular, open, and honest dinner-table conversations, is that she felt she really knew her children—how they thought, how they felt, and what was important to them.

"Professionals who work with families know the importance of a sense of belonging to an individual," writes Judith Martin. "They work with many adults who are spending a lifetime searching for a sense of family in some of the most unexpected places: work, chemicals, cults, movements, the military, or even multiple marriages."[4]

Katy has spent four years as a houseparent at a residential community for people in transition. "We wouldn't have community here if it weren't for our evening meals," observes Katy. "Programs don't work. We've tried things like reading devotions. What works is letting them talk. We'll ask 'Who has something they're thankful for, or a prayer request?' Someone will pop up and say 'I have a new job!' and the whole room will cheer." Some of the 24 residents sit in the same spot each night and some move around. Almost none of them have grown up with family interaction around a table, and it is therapeutic for them.

When Holly's husband Wayne died in an accident leaving behind Holly and their three children, Holly said the hardest thing for months was sitting down with the children to eat dinner without Wayne. Mealtimes had been the key to their sense of family identity: "This is who we are together." Then Holly had to painstakingly build a new sense of family identity: "This is *now* who we are together. We must think of ourselves as a family, as a whole."

The same challenge faces single parents. They must learn to look at the family remnant who sit at their table as the new whole. This new, whole family

needs the warmth and security of a consistent table time to work through everyday situations as well as the changes in their lives.

Even singles and couples with no children, and those who have never married, can enrich their own identity and better appreciate the identity of families around them by understanding the importance of table time for themselves as well as for others. As an example, one group of Christian college students who lived in several units of a 16-unit apartment building would pool their meager resources once a month, buy as much food as they could afford, and feast together around a common table, enjoying God's provision of fine food and loving fellowship. Twenty years later, many of those men and women look back at that experience as the foundation for quality mealtimes with their own growing families today.

No matter what its form, the family that meets together and eats together will have a whole lot of fun. Mimi and her family first spread their table in a mobile home, then on an Indian reservation in New Mexico, then in Colorado, in Africa, in Peru, in Quito, and in the jungles of Ecuador. All those dinnertimes together have built sentimental, serious, and silly memories to cherish as family members now live continents apart.

Flexible consistency is the key to making the most of family mealtimes. The food does not have to be fancy or time-consuming to prepare—it simply needs to be reasonably nutritious.

We don't expect great things every mealtime. Our family dinner next Thursday night may seem uneventful. Perhaps the following Thursday I'll accidentally burn the meat and the boys will argue. But we believe that the practice of the family meal, over time, can build character, security, and wonderful memories.

Americans love to poke fun at *Leave It to Beaver* and at June Cleaver greeting the family in her high heels and pearls. But the Cleavers's frequent dinner table scenes show us something to envy: regular family dinners where Beaver spills the beans, problems unravel, and everyone talks about the day. We see the Cleavers as a family, as a team, gathered around a dining room table with a white tablecloth.

Enjoy the family you love. Don't sacrifice getting to know one another well just because you're busy; someday the kids will be gone—time does run out.

But for now, find the particular mealtimes when your family is most able to consistently eat together. Develop a meal preparation plan that works for you. (At the end of each chapter of this book we give menu suggestions, and in chapter 4 we discuss meal planning techniques. *A ▼ beside a menu item indicates a recipe that appears in the back of the book.* We also include some ideas to spark fresh dinner table conversation.) Figure out how to get the family to help. Then grab that time—through soccer season, Grandma's visit, or Dad's evening class— shifting nights and mealtimes as necessary.

And don't give up the fight for quality family time!

▾ CHAPTER 2 ▾

WELCOME HOME

We all crave a home where
we're welcomed and accepted
for who we are.

After Hurricane Andrew devastated South Florida in 1992, national television news showed people camping in wrecked homes without roofs, running water, or electricity. "Why do you stay?" they were asked. "Because it's home," they said. Home is that important to every one of us.

But to be truly home it must be a refuge. The busier we are, the more we need a center of rest and connection at home. That's the challenge for the wise woman of Proverbs who builds her home. She is building a refuge brick by brick, with love and patience. Persistence is the mortar which holds the finished structure together.[1]

In a home that's a refuge, chores can wait a few moments while a child strokes and confides in a cat. A father can watch television with a bowl of popcorn in his lap and choose not to answer the phone. A mother can relax in the tub undisturbed while her worries melt away.

A home that is a refuge is where you want to be, where you know your family is glad you're there. It's a sanctuary where you can retreat and lick your wounds from the battle outside; a place where you can wear that comfy old flannel shirt with holes in the elbows.

If home is not a refuge, family members will find a refuge somewhere else—at a friend's house, at the office, at a restaurant, at a bar, in a gang—wherever they feel welcome just as they are.

The welcome is important. With a slap of the screen door a child enters from the backyard, his imagination returning from the moon. A teenage daughter sulks because she has just argued with her boyfriend. Dad suffers from an Excedrin headache and a futile-feeling day. Mom is exhausted from a meeting and just wants to take off her shoes and relax. They all need and appreciate an accepting welcome, no matter from how near or far they've come. They want their presence not only to be acknowledged, but to be appreciated.

Why should we fuss over a guest at the door but fail to acknowledge when a loved one enters? Every home needs at least one person with the mental energy to focus on the needs of each family member separate from the logistical running of the household. That person is custodian of the welcome, taking care to see there is one. It is a difficult job to create an island of peace, and it doesn't happen without someone's special effort. But when family members feel welcome in their own home, they are more likely to want to share their home with guests.

In Mimi's home in Quito, the ceilings are high and the dark wood floors are cool. Narrow courtyard gardens encircle the house, so that each window reveals a striking glimpse of the profusion of flowers outside. There is always music in the house, either classical music or hymns of worship. It's a place where it is hard be cranky, and where family members and guests alike sleep well. In the front hall just inside the door a pegboard is mounted on the wall. Each peg holds a different bright miniature felt hat like those worn by Indians in Ecuador. It's the symbol, says Mimi, that little people are welcome in the Wilson home, and she points it out to all children who enter.

Of course, because of work schedules, classes, appointments, or errands, some of us can't always be there when our children get home. But we can still leave an aura of welcome and care. We can leave notes ("Here are the packets of hot chocolate we'll share this evening when I get home"); we can leave a simple "treasure map" to a snack; or we can at least call home from work to check on them.

Many of us naturally wither when we don't sense a welcome. One group of high-risk teenagers was asked what they most wished was different at home, and they said they wished someone was there to ask how their day went. When someone was at home it was more often "Where the heck have you been?" than "Hi, how are you?"

It's important for parents to be available when kids want to talk. Kids don't talk on demand. Where and when do your kids talk? Tune in to when and where it is. Chances are it's in the kitchen, and at mealtime, where much of their time is spent and many of their needs are met.

A nutritious, predictable evening mealtime goes far in creating a home that's a refuge. When I was growing up in Topeka, Kansas, we ate dinner every night as soon as Walter Cronkite signed off from the 6:00 o'clock news. Every night we sat down to meat with gravy or ketchup, potatoes, a vegetable, milk, and white bread with butter. It was tasty, consistent, and we were there.

Since then, more has changed than the typical menu. It's not easy any more to consistently pull off a meal. (In chapter 4 we'll look at ways to simplify meal preparation.) The real challenge, however, is enticing a busy family to the table and making it a place they want to linger a while. So here are a few tips:

Eat at a table, eye-to-eye, one which is properly set for at least one meal of the day. There is a psychology to table setting. A set table sends the message, "We are all going to sit down and eat. We hope you can join us. You don't need to snack too much because there's something big planned for you." A completely set table eliminates the annoying practice of jumping up from the table to fetch napkins or more milk. A set table also says, "Don't drop your backpack or the mail here. I'm occupied."

Some families find it more convenient to stack plates and pile utensils in the middle of the table with everyone then taking what is needed. Other families find paper tableware a great convenience. An ad for one brand of paperware reads, "Solo Cups, Plates And Refills Make Every Day Feel Like A Vacation." Maybe so, but some days it's good to use real dishes and feel like we're not on vacation. After all, we're at home.

Just as kids can get by with slip-on shoes but also need to learn the skill of tying laces, so too, kids need to learn the skill of setting a table. Of course, the set table doesn't always have to be the one in the kitchen or dining room. Eating Chinese-style, on your knees at a coffee table, works just fine. So does a table on the patio, on a balcony, or in a park; eating on a blanket in the yard after dark; or even from TV trays in front of a fireplace. Variety is refreshing.

Although freshly-cut flowers make a lovely centerpiece, anything attractive or interesting will do: fresh vegetables from the market, ceramic bunnies off a window ledge, a child's Lego creation, a small stuffed animal or toy, a basket of shiny apples. Assign a family member to choose a centerpiece. Or, for a cultural experience, buy an unusual fruit and place it in a special dish in the center of the table. "Does anyone know what it is? Where it grows?" "Why haven't we eaten this before?" Then cut it up and eat it for dessert.

Use candles often. We were invited for dinner one evening to the home of a dear woman who loves to cook and give dinner parties but has outlived peers to entertain. She asked our boys not only to light the many candles down the center of her dining room table, but also—to my horror—those in the wall sconces. She showed them how she had ingeniously covered the burned places on the wallpaper.

Candlelight is mystical. People linger at a table to talk in the candlelight. It softens faces and foods and blurs the edges of what could have been sharp remarks. Although younger children may become preoccupied with putting their fingers in the wax or lighting and snuffing out the candles, they, too, are drawn into the dreamy mood.

If you have special china, use it now and then for an occasion no more special than to communicate that your family is worth the best. Why is it that we would die for our children, but we won't use our best china for them? Who is worthy of our best things if they aren't? Mimi uses her good china often. She's told her children they will inherit her china, but not to expect full sets. In place of a few broken pieces they'll savor the memories of a lot of meals eaten and enjoyed together.

Use a special plate—even just a different plate bought at a garage sale—to celebrate a family member's achievement, a kindness, or an admirable character quality. In our family someone receives the special plate each Sunday morning, but our rule is that a child cannot ask to receive it.

Eat together. A standard family dinnertime is an important frame of reference. All family members should know to be home at the standard time you set or to call a half hour before it if they will be late. The idea is to avoid the I-didn't-know-dinner-was-at-6:00 routine.

There will be times when dinner must be postponed. Young children (teenagers, too) will need a snack of fruit or yogurt so they won't get crabby. Sure there will be times when mealtime is missed all together or when only part of the family will share a meal, but as much as possible, activities should be planned around that special half- to three-quarters of an hour. One writer observes, "Specific conversations are beside the point: It is the cumulative memories that count. What stays with us most from those innumerable family mealtimes is the feeling of knowing how important we all are to one another—important enough to make us stop everything, disengage from the outside world, and gather round the dinner table to share our lives."[2]

Turn off the telephone and television. Odds are a dinnertime phone call is either selling carpet cleaning or requesting a donation, so don't answer it. If it is important, the caller will leave a message or call back.

As for the television, which has been called "the new hearth," there's no greater conversation buster.

A *Reader's Digest* article reports that "a New York Times/CBS News poll showed that among families with children under age 18 living at home, 42 percent spend the dinner hour watching TV. Even worse, kids who microwave their own dinners and chow down in front of the TV set lose the sense that family is more important than TV time."[3]

If it's important to watch the news, schedule dinner to follow it so you can discuss together what you heard. If someone must see a dinnertime show, videotape it for viewing later. Don't become better acquainted with a sitcom family at their dinner table than you are with your own family at yours.

Needless to say, the same goes for portable stereos and newspapers. If someone in your family is hopelessly attached, gently but firmly persuade him to forgo it for certain times on which you stake the claim of family mealtime. Hopefully it won't take too long for him to see the advantage and pleasure of tuning in to the family instead.

In a home that is a refuge, family members feel welcome and mealtimes feel secure. I remember our dinners in the dead of winter when Alex was unemployed. There was something about the contrast between the blackness outside our windows and the warmth of the five of us gathered around our table—with enough food, one another, and faith in a God who cared for us.

Every evening's meal doesn't have to meet a particular standard in menu, in conversation, or in length of time at the table. But with priority status and consistency, our mealtimes will create a sense of security and a home refuge.

Nutmeg Muffins

2 cups flour
1 ½ cups brown sugar, packed
⅓ cup margarine
1 cup flour
2 teaspoons baking powder
2 teaspoons nutmeg
½ teaspoon baking soda
½ teaspoon salt
1 cup buttermilk
2 eggs, slightly beaten

Preheat oven to 350°. Mix the 2 cups flour and the brown sugar in medium-sized bowl. Cut in margarine with two knives until mixture resembles coarse cornmeal. Reserve ¾ cup of the mixture for topping. Add 1 cup flour, baking powder, nutmeg, soda, and salt to remaining mixture in bowl. Add buttermilk and eggs, stirring just until moistened. Spoon batter into well greased muffin cups, half full. Sprinkle each muffin with 1 heaping teaspoon of the topping. Bake at 350° 20 minutes or until wooden pick inserted into center comes out clean. Makes 1 ½ dozen medium-sized muffins. Yummy with potato soup and apple slices, or for breakfast with fruit.

Tea at Ten
Nutmeg Muffins
Decaffeinated herbal tea

Table Talk:
Tell about one thing you started today and one thing you finished.

Treasure Hunt
After School Snack
A bag of microwave popcorn to pop
Apple cider or juice

Table Talk:
When I get home tell me the answer to this riddle: What did the big computer say to the small computer? Answer: You're a chip off the old block.

Refrigerator Bran Muffins

Sunday Morning Breakfast

Refrigerator Bran Muffins (Prepare batter Saturday night)

Scrambled eggs

Coffee and orange juice

Bacon or sausage (optional)

Table Talk:

Pray the Lord's Prayer, taking turns with the phrases around the table (learning it if not everyone knows it). What does it mean to you that God is your Father?

1 cup boiling water
1 cup bran
1 ¾ cups sugar
½ cup vegetable shortening
2 eggs
2 ½ cups all-purpose flour
2 ½ teaspoons baking soda
½ teaspoon salt
1 ¾ cups buttermilk
2 cups All-Bran cereal
¾ cup golden raisins

Pour boiling water over bran. Let stand until cool. Cream sugar and shortening. Add eggs one at a time. Sift dry ingredients and add alternately with buttermilk. Beat until smooth. Add cooled bran, All-Bran, and raisins. Refrigerate overnight. Do not stir. Fill muffin tins half full. Bake 20 minutes at 400°. Batter keeps 4-5 weeks in refrigerator. Makes 3 dozen muffins.

Impassable* Chicken Parmigiana Pie

¾ cup low-fat cottage cheese
⅓ cup grated Parmesan cheese
1 ½ cups cooked chicken, boned and diced
1 ¼ cups shredded mozzarella cheese
½ teaspoon garlic powder
½ teaspoon oregano
½ teaspoon basil
¼ teaspoon pepper
1 6-ounce can tomato paste
1 cup milk
2 eggs
⅔ cup baking mix (i.e. Bisquick)

Spray a 10-inch pie plate with nonstick spray. Layer cottage cheese and Parmesan cheese in pie plate. Mix chicken, ½ cup mozzarella cheese, garlic powder, oregano, basil, pepper, and tomato paste. Spoon over Parmesan cheese. Beat the milk, eggs, and baking mix in a blender on high speed for 15 seconds or until smooth. Pour into pie plate and bake at 400° for 30 minutes. Top with remaining mozzarella cheese. Bake 8-10 minutes longer or until knife inserted comes out clean. Let cool for 5 minutes. Cut into 6-8 servings.

* The title, originally "Impossible," is due to my son Dan's typo. We liked it.

Family Dinner
Impassable Chicken Parmigiana Pie with Broccoli or
▼ Impossible Garden Pie
Fresh fruit
▼ Chocolate Chip Cake

Table Talk:
Think up some questions and play Family Trivia. For example, how did Mom and Dad meet? What was the name of our first family pet? How many second cousins do you have and what are their names?

Family Dinner

▼ Chicken with a Zip
Parmesan Potatoes
Carrots, cooked
or fresh
Dessert: star fruit,
mango, or any fruit
unknown to
your family

Table Talk:

Is there any part of our
home that you are afraid of
in the dark? Where do you
not like to be in the dark?

Family Dinner

Crispy Potato Quiche
Frozen Salad
Cookies

Table Talk:

What makes our home
feel homiest to you?

Parmesan Potatoes

2 tablespoons margarine
4 large red potatoes
⅓ cup grated Parmesan cheese
2 tablespoons flour
½ teaspoon salt
¼ teaspoon paprika
¼ teaspoon pepper

Melt margarine in 9x9-inch baking dish. Cut the potatoes into
bite-size pieces. Put remaining ingredients in a lock-top bag.
Shake potatoes in cheese mixture, coating well. Place potatoes in
baking dish and bake at 350°, turning once, for 50 minutes or
until brown.

Crispy Potato Quiche

1 24-ounce package frozen shredded hash browns, thawed
¼ cup melted butter
¾ cup shredded hot pepper cheese
1 cup shredded Swiss cheese
1 cup diced cooked ham
½ cup half and half
2 eggs
¼ teaspoon seasoned salt

Press thawed hash browns between paper towels to remove moisture. Press hash browns into greased 10-inch pie plate, to form a solid crust. Brush with melted butter, making certain to brush top edges. Bake at 425° for 25 minutes. Remove from oven. Sprinkle cheeses and ham evenly over hash brown crust. Beat half and half with eggs and seasoned salt. Pour over cheeses and ham. Bake uncovered at 350° for 30-40 minutes or until knife inserted in center comes out clean. Serves 6.

Frozen Salad

2 cups sour cream
2 tablespoons lemon juice
¼ cup sugar
⅛ teaspoon salt
1 20-ounce can crushed pineapple, drained
¼ cup maraschino cherries, diced
¼ cup pecans or walnuts, chopped
1 banana, diced
¼ teaspoon vanilla

Stir all ingredients together. Spoon into muffin liners in muffin tins and freeze. Pop out and store in freezer in a lock-top bag. Remove as many muffins as you want to serve, allowing them to thaw slightly. Makes 1 ½ dozen.

CHAPTER 3

TABLE TALK

Conversational skills learned
around the family table carry over
to the classroom, and into adult life.

I could recite all the American presidents when I was in kindergarten, and I still can," a young woman proudly told me. Her parents made a game of learning at the dinner table, creating silly rhythms with the initials of the presidents' names to help their children memorize them.

In contrast, an elementary school principal recently said, "I really notice the difference in our kindergartners over the years. They lack vocabulary. They aren't able to carry on a conversation. I think it's because they sit in front of the TV so much and aren't talked to by their parents at home."

Children learn conversational skills in the course of family discussions. When conversation doesn't happen in the home, children have difficulty conversing with adults, and sometimes even with their peers. When conversation does happen, they learn skills that carry over into school and into life. A recent *USA Today*/CNN/Gallup poll on factors contributing to happiness and high marks in school included these findings: Religious students with strong family support are the most likely to succeed in school. A related factor is that the most successful students were also those most likely to eat dinner regularly with the whole family.[1]

Dolores Curran also sees the effect of family table talk on children at school: "Teachers often are able to identify students who come from such families. These students seem confident that their opinions are respected, even if they aren't shared. The give-and-take of good family discussion is valuable for another reason: It gives children practice in articulating their thoughts at home so that eventually they'll feel confident outside the home."[2]

Each of us needs a forum where we can express without censor our dreams, our irrational fears, and our crazy ideas. We need a place where people bear with

our jokes even if they've heard them many times or if they're not funny. We need a place where we don't have to be the smartest or the funniest, where what we have to say is of value.

A friend reminisced about her son's days in kindergarten: "I loved those days when Rob thought he could do anything and the world hadn't yet taught him he couldn't." The world will, indeed, tell each of us that we can't always accomplish our dreams. We don't need to learn that at the dinner table. Rather, we need the reinforcement to keep trying!

The characters and chemistry in each family are unique. There's no pat formula to get them all talking. But a few tips will help ensure success.

▼ Setting the Stage ▼

1. Sit down together at the table and keep distractions, especially the television and telephone, at a minimum.

2. Treat each family member with respect. Establish ground rules regarding monopolizing the conversation. If someone loves center stage, jump in when he or she pauses for a breath and ask someone else to comment.

Mimi has spent much time in Quito listening carefully to conversations in Spanish, trying to understand and figure out how to respond. In her listening, she's learned to tell the difference between people who are merely taking turns talking and those who are really communicating. Too often we listen with our minds preoccupied with our own response. But when communication, the real connection, takes place, it's awesome. And it's worth wading through many other family discussions to get there!

3. Establish some basic rules concerning acceptable table language, behavior, and topics. One morning during a cholera epidemic in a jungle area of Ecuador, the Wilson family was eating breakfast in the hotel dining room, discussing the characteristics of choleric symptoms. A doctor and his family in the midst of an epidemic can get away with that, but most of us can't.

4. Children should ask to be excused and should learn to sit at the table for a reasonable length of time, according to their age and personality, after they have finished eating. For young children, coloring books at the table can help keep their minds and hands occupied.

5. Steer the conversation away from criticizing other people, whether present or absent. Although we don't condone everyone's behavior, we should uphold each person's worth. If this is the general attitude displayed toward people through the talk around the table, children will feel safe expressing their own feelings. If a child or adult expresses strong feelings—for example, disappointment over failing a test—empathize rather than criticize. Don't make light of it, think of excuses, or blame the teacher for being unreasonable.

6. Ask questions at the table for which anyone seated will have an answer, and which cannot be answered with simply yes or no. Set the tone by being honest and vulnerable. For example, if a child is experiencing a rough ride through puberty, reminisce about your own experiences at that age. Let your child know you didn't feel secure about yourself, or that you didn't make it to adulthood without suffering some scrapes along the way.

7. Colossians 4:6 (NAS) says, "Let your speech always be with grace, seasoned, as it were, with salt, so that you may know how you should respond to each person." Using just the right amount of salt doesn't call attention to the

saltiness or the lack of saltiness in food, but it enhances natural flavors. Let your conversation bring out the best in others. Be animated but not sharp. Participate but don't dominate.

Just out of college, Alex studied at L'Abri, a Christian retreat in England. Twenty years later he remembers three things: working in the garden (which he hated), listening to tapes while wrapped in a blanket in a drafty room, and engaging in spirited dinner table conversations.

So what is there to talk about in your home? Plenty!

You can plan a discussion question or two, or just let it flow. Chances are over time you'll use a good mix of both. Encourage children to participate on their own levels of understanding.

Mimi calls planned discussion "putting a subject on the table." When you do this, remember the objective is to get everyone thinking and sharing from their own experiences and insights. The point is not to reach a consensus or the "correct" answer.

Good topic ideas can surface from other conversations, books, newspaper or magazine articles, movies or TV shows, political speeches, or neighborhood issues. When a good idea comes to mind, write it on the calendar or a chalkboard in the kitchen. Or put it on a Post-it note at your place at the table so you won't forget it. Sometimes assign other family members to come up with the questions.

Following are some ideas for discussion. They are categorized under general motives with which we might approach family discussions: for fun, education, family devotions, teaching values, family meetings, and getting to know guests.

When we believe each family member has something unique to contribute, we become detectives, searching for the right questions to ask.

▼ Just for Fun ▼

We would all like family time together around the table to be a time we look forward to, a time that is relaxed and fun. How does it become that way? One way is by parents focusing attention on the family. Mealtime is not the time for ponderous discussions about what's happening at work. Meals are fun if we build a mix of predictable traditions everyone enjoys and pepper these with variety and the unexpected.

Families with a distinctive sense of humor often have developed it from shared experiences during table time. Kevin and Kyndra Wilson like to bring a book by Erma Bombeck or Dave Barry to the table and have family members take turns reading aloud. They also read aloud at restaurants while they wait for their food.

Make Dad or a teenage son the "answer man" and Mom or a teenage daughter the "answer woman." Each child can ask one question to try to stump the answer man or woman. A creative answer suffices as well as a correct one, thus chances are you'll all be amazed how much the answer man or woman "knows"!

Read excerpts from a letter addressed to the family and reminisce about those particular relatives or friends. Pray for them. Compose a round-robin reply, with each person adding a few lines.

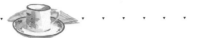

Bring a cartoon, riddle, joke, or poem to the table.

If a conversation falls flat, so what? Try another one.

Our middle-school-age son doesn't like to linger long at the table. When he wants to be excused, I might say, "Not until you've told us one funny thing that happened to you at school today."

"Well," he might say, "someone set off a bottle rocket in the hall next to my locker." (Sometimes what they think is funny may not be too funny to you! Oh, well.)

▾ For Education ▾

The potential for education for a captive audience of two or three generations is exciting, especially when kids see that their parents can learn from children as well as from other adults.

When famine and civil war gripped Somalia and the United Nations sent troops and food, we pulled out the family atlas—a good resource to keep near the table. Where is Somalia, anyway? Perhaps a child knows and an adult doesn't. What countries does it border? What are its climate and topography? What have we learned about the situation there? One six-year-old girl reflected on the situation in Somalia at her family dinner table: "Too bad Somalia doesn't have a Joseph. He prepared for famine."

Put a globe in the center of the table and make a game of finding particular countries, oceans, seas, large cities, or continents. Study a chart of the constellations visible at that time of year. Choose three or four in particular and then search the sky for them later that night. Curiosity is contagious; pass it on.

The world is shrinking rapidly through the elimination of political barriers and through advances in communication and travel. Our children are likely to venture farther into the world than we have, at the least by linking electronically with people of other cultures. At the table, families can share knowledge and skills that will help prepare children for life in their world.

If a child is studying a foreign language, or if a parent knows another language, learn as a family some common words and expressions. Discuss how that language differs from English. Learn the gracious words: *thank you; please; excuse me; good morning.*

During presidential elections, *Weekly Reader* publishes predictions based upon a survey of their readers, who are children. Children usually reflect their parents' preferences. Where do they learn their parents' preferences? Probably at the table.

The election process can be confusing even for adults. Discuss at the table, at a level appropriate for the children's ages, political parties, major issues and positions of candidates, the electoral college, and the democratic republic as a form of government. Allow and encourage good debate (that is, no one is allowed to monopolize). Require everyone to defend his or her position.

Plan a mealtime or snack to share while the family watches presidential debates. How often are we or our children exposed to polished public address? Discuss afterward what you heard, what stirred you, with what you agreed or disagreed. Talk about the manners of presentation.

Discuss movies or musical performances the whole family has seen; do the same with books. Encourage family members to think, analyze, and articulate with the goal of discerning the precious and recognizing the worthless.

Children must learn that not everything in print is worth reading. Not everything on television is worth watching. Not everything seen and heard in the various media is true or healthy. Not all adults are trustworthy, nor their conduct worth emulating.

Define words and concepts: urban versus suburban, civil rights, abortion, freedom of speech, freedom of religion, salvation by works or by grace. Katie Couric, NBC-TV "Today" show coanchor, says she grew up in a home where her dad asked each of his four children to bring a new word to the table each night.

Discuss a child's writing assignment with questions like, "How do you think you'll approach that?" "What have you learned on this topic?" "What do you want your readers to learn?" Verbalizing the main idea will help a child write more clearly.

▼ For Family Devotions ▼

According to Bruce Wilkinson, author of *The Family Walk*, there is no topic that incites more frustration in the Christian mother or more guilt in the Christian father than that of family devotions.[3]

In his extensive travels over 30 years, Dr. Harold Westing, associate professor of pastoral ministries at Denver Seminary, has stayed in homes instead of hotels whenever possible. During his visits in hundreds of homes, he has learned there are basically two ways families teach children about Christianity: as a system or as a relationship.

Teaching spiritual principles is most effective when they are delivered in the warp and woof of life, in the course of everyday conversation, like answering the question "Where did you see God working in your life today?" Instead of merely teaching commandments, we might share personal encounters with God and His commandments, teaching that God is a Person and teaching a reverence for His attributes.

Don't exclude God talk from the fun talk you have at the table. Don't relegate it to only a set apart, solemn time. If you read a family devotional or passages of Scripture at the table, or perhaps memorize Bible verses, keep the time brief, the focus relevant, your prayers genuine, and don't be afraid to have fun.

Use object lessons. Place a jar of yeast and water in the center of the table and ask "What does this have to do with the Bible?"[4] Place a cheese grater on the table and ask, "What verse in the Bible does this remind you of?" (*Greater* is He who is in you than he who is in the world.[5] *Greater* love has no one than this, that one lay down his life for his friends.[6]) As you use the salt shaker ask, "Who can think of ways salt is mentioned in the Bible?" (Let your speech always . . . be seasoned with salt.[7] You are the salt of the earth.[8] [Lot's]wife . . . became a pillar of salt.[9])

Steve, a youth pastor we know, is an athlete. When one of our sons bragged about his ability in a particular sport, Steve casually referred to Luke 2:52: "You know," he said, "Jesus grew in wisdom mentally; in stature physically; and in favor with God spiritually; and with men socially. That's the balanced life we should strive for."

If guests are present, you might ask "How would you describe your spiritual pilgrimage?" Ask this of several different guests over time and you will begin to notice repeated responses and aspects of God's character. (The Wilsons have noted that long before the soul of a man responds to God, God is at work in his life.)

Don't keep God in a box; include Him at the table.

▼   For Teaching Values   ▼

Use your conversation to help children appreciate values that are not specific to the American dream, but cross lines of culture and standards of living. For example, commend people who exemplify resourcefulness, honesty, generosity, and perseverance. When the Wilsons were in Africa, Mimi discovered that a woman returning from her garden in the jungle had filled three-year-old Kevin's overalls pocket with freshly dug peanuts. As Mimi cleaned the mud from around Kevin's mouth, she wondered what type of parasites he might have acquired. Noting the apprehension in his mother's eyes, Kevin tried to alleviate her fears: "But Mom, she was only being kind!"

In a profile in *Life* magazine, a man who had served as doorman at the White House for many years described his work. In his words, "I caught on to it pretty fast, but I also felt that the work could be done with more dignity. I asked to be given the name of anyone that I was going to meet—I didn't care who it was—and when I met that person, even if it was a maid coming about a job, I would greet him or her by name. And while I was escorting the people we would just talk. By the time we got where we were going, their nervousness would be quieted and they would be calm enough to meet whomever it was they were frightened to death to meet."[10]

Discuss stories that show character. Conversely, also discuss newspaper articles that show the consequences of negative traits such as sensuality or greed.

▾ For Family Meetings ▾

Mealtime can be used for a periodic family meeting. At your meetings discuss family rules—especially at the beginning of a new school year—regarding homework, bedtimes, and television; at the beginning of summer, plan a vacation or activities; or anytime discuss a problem the family needs to handle collectively.

At a family meeting you might decide the appropriate gift the family will give at an upcoming wedding, birthday, or graduation celebration.

Think of a neighbor, relative, or friend who could use some encouragement and in what ways you as a family could help. Fix a meal, watch pets, baby-sit, mow the lawn, give flowers, and so on. Soon after Christmas, hold a family meeting for the purpose of writing thank-you notes.

Family meetings can teach children appropriate (and inappropriate) questions to ask upcoming guests, saving everyone involved possible hurt and embarrassment. The Wilsons often entertain guests who are suffering, either physically or emotionally. Their children learned early that asking, "Why did your husband beat you?" is not appropriate. Children also can learn when it's appropriate to ask questions, and when they should listen but not talk. They can also learn to model their parents' behavior in keeping conversations confidential. This not only teaches children sensitivity to people's needs and feelings, it helps them trust enough to share their own.

▾ With Guests ▾

Plan table talk questions when you're expecting company for a meal. If the conversation flows easily and you don't need to use the questions, great. If not, making a game of it can put everyone at ease.

We often use questions from The Ungame, with one question placed face down at each place at the table. If your children like to help, let them write place cards for each person. Questions can then be written on the inside of each place card. This icebreaker works especially well when one person at the table might otherwise dominate the conversation.

Often questions will be just for fun, like, "What is your favorite room in your home and why?" Or, "If you could spend a day with anyone in the world, who would it be?"

If you are hosting a mix of people who are used to having ideas questioned and won't take it personally, you can go deeper. Often you will want to play to the strength or expertise of your guest(s).

Cal and Mimi had a dinner party to honor the visiting parents of some close friends. Several people were invited in addition to the guests of honor. Mimi knew her guests were a widely-respected, devoted couple. Her question for the wife was this: "How have you maintained romance in your marriage all these years?" For the husband it was: "How can we live a godly life despite the world's temptations?" She had discussed the questions with the couple in advance, so their answers were instructive to everyone at the table.

If you have a Trivial Pursuit game, read questions to the group. Often you will learn more about the people present than about the trivia!

Vary what happens at the table so your time is a routine, yet far from boring. Heated discussions are okay, often stimulating, as long as family members treat one another's opinions with respect.

Parents set the tone at the table. They must forge an undercurrent of respect, and they must be willing to listen. "One of the major causes of stress in families is not feeling heard or acknowledged."[11] While parents may have the final say, it's important that children feel their ideas are valued and that they participate in family decisions. When they do, the family is richer, the family's sense of identity is stronger, and the children are better equipped to participate with confidence in the classroom and in their world.

I asked one mother of six whether her family all participated in dinner table discussions. She replied, "My rule is, Be quiet and eat!" Sometimes I can empathize, but as a general rule, let's get them talking!

Slow Cooker Cobbler

4 medium-sized tart apples, peeled and sliced
¼ cup honey
1 teaspoon cinnamon
2 tablespoons margarine, melted
2 cups low-fat granola cereal

Place apples in slow cooker and mix in remaining ingredients.
Cover and cook on low 7-9 hours (overnight) or on high
2-3 hours. Serve with milk. Serves 4.

Mexican Meat Loaf

1 egg, beaten
¼ cup water
2 teaspoons chili powder
½ teaspoon salt
½ teaspoon cumin
1 8-ounce can refried beans
1 tablespoon onion, minced
1 2 ¼-ounce can sliced pitted ripe olives (use ½ can)
1 ½ pounds lean ground beef
½ cup cheddar cheese, shredded

In a mixing bowl combine the egg, water, chili powder, salt,
and cumin. Add beans, onion, and olives and mix well.
Add ground beef; mix thoroughly with hands. Freeze at this

Tea at Ten
English muffins
with jam
Decaffeinated
herbal tea

Table Talk:
What was your
favorite childhood
storybook? Why did
you like it?

Breakfast
Slow Cooker
Cobbler
Grapefruit halves

Table Talk:
If you could spend one
whole day with a good
friend, who would that
friend be and what
would you do?

47

Family Dinner

Mexican Meat Loaf

Rice-a-Roni Spanish Rice mix, substituting 1 14 ½-ounce can Mexican-style stewed tomatoes

▼ Easy Fruit Dessert

Table Talk:

Ask someone ahead of time to bring a favorite poem to the table and read it. Discuss the poem. Of what do its images remind you?

Family Dinner

▼ Janie's Chicken Breasts

Roasted Red Potatoes

Green beans

▼ Pumpkin Chip Cookies

point if desired, with the cheese frozen in a separate bag and taped to the meat loaf container.

Pat mixture firmly into ungreased 5 ½-cup ring mold. Turn meat out of ring onto broiling pan with slits and an under-pan to catch grease. Bake at 350° for 45 minutes.

Sprinkle cheese on top of loaf. Bake 5 minutes more or until cheese melts. Remove loaf to serving platter. To serve, fill center of ring with shredded lettuce and tomato wedges. Serves 6-8.

You can double this recipe and freeze one (or both). Serve with Rice-a-Roni Spanish Rice mix prepared according to package directions, but substituting a 14 ½-ounce can Mexican-style stewed tomatoes for the diced tomatoes.

Roasted Red Potatoes

16 medium unpeeled red potatoes, scrubbed and quartered
(about 2 ½ pounds)
2 tablespoons vegetable oil
¾ teaspoon garlic powder
¾ teaspoon onion powder
½ teaspoon salt
⅛ teaspoon cayenne pepper
⅛ teaspoon paprika

Place potatoes in a 13x9x2-inch baking pan. Mix remaining ingredients, and drizzle over potatoes stirring until potatoes are thoroughly coated. Bake at 400° for 1 hour or until lightly browned, stirring after 30 minutes. Serves 6-8.

Winter Pot Roast

4-pound chuck roast
2 tablespoons steak sauce
2 medium onions, sliced
2 8-ounce cans tomato sauce
1 cup catsup
1 teaspoon salt
1 teaspoon sugar
¼ teaspoon pepper
1 ½ tablespoons prepared horseradish
1 12-ounce package wide egg noodles
Optional: *1 tablespoon caraway seeds*

Put everything but last two ingredients in crockpot and cook on low for 10 hours, or on high 5 hours. Shred meat with a fork. Serve over wide egg noodles that have been cooked, drained, and tossed with caraway seeds. Top with some of the sauce in the crockpot. Serves 6.

Table Talk:
(Family meeting) Discuss household emergencies. What would you do if there was fire in the house? Where and how do you turn off water to the house if necessary? How do you call the fire department or police? How do you fix an overflowing toilet? (After dinner!)

Family Dinner
Winter Pot Roast
Tossed green salad
Ice cream sundaes

Table Talk:
Where did you see God's presence in your life today?

49

CHAPTER 4

OVEN TO TABLE

Meal planning is a critical
investment of time.

Two families, related by marriage, spend two weeks together every summer at a cabin on a lake. The three generations and 23 people overflow into neighboring cottages to sleep, but they eat dinners together in the living room of the main cabin at two large tables with a high chair or two at the ends. The cousins, aunts, uncles, and grandparents share more than a meal. They share more togetherness than most extended families will ever know. And after the dishes are cleared away, at least one table full of assorted ages stays to play a game.

Dinner for 23 takes planning. The women plan menus together and the families rotate chores. But there's no question all the work is worth it.

Planning for our own day-in, day-out family meals is not so much fun, but it's worth the time, too. Careful planning eliminates mental anxiety, which accounts for more than half the energy we expend preparing a meal.

In a survey conducted by the National Potato Board, women from across the country were asked to express their feelings about the dinner hour by drawing a picture. "One drawing showed a woman at the bottom of a tornado, while another featured a time bomb to illustrate her emotions concerning mealtime preparations. Other survey findings: More than 50 percent of respondents are spending more than one hour to prepare dinner. Forty-two percent would like to spend a half hour to one hour, yet only 20 percent are able to do so."[1]

The person responsible for managing family meals plays out a dynamic tension between her lack of time, energy, money, and cooking talents and her desire to consistently provide nutritious meals for her family. To keep this tension at bay, she must do three things: She must stay in touch with her own limits; she must invest the time necessary to develop a meal plan; and she must remain flexible and willing to change the plan when the family schedule or a change in eating habits causes the meal plan to break down.

▾ Set the Pace ▾

In a sense, moms are like balloons. We start the day blown up, with the goal of planning our day so that we can let out air slowly through the day and still have some left for the evening. To do that we must know our limits.

Many of us are used to comparing ourselves with others. We want someone else's energy level, but we are unaware of our own strengths and weaknesses. It takes time to find our level of calmness. That level is the state of mind and body at which we function best for the long haul. And that level is the place of mind where children can act like children—spill milk, ask the 15,000th question of the day about ants—and you don't lose it emotionally if your husband asks a favor. Most of us feel that unless we are wound tight, unless every moment is filled, we are not using our time wisely. But that sort of life is not peak performance. Peak performance occurs when we find our level of calmness and function within it.

We alone are responsible for pacing ourselves and for noticing what recharges us. A hot bath? A change of shoes or makeup? A walk after dinner? Soothing music? A few minutes in a good book? Tea from a tea set kept in our bedroom? Reading the newspaper? We must make time regularly for whatever refreshes us. If not for our own sakes, we must do it for the sake of those with whom we live and work.

▼ Invest In Planning ▼

Meal planning time is an investment that keeps the day from unraveling for us and the whole family three-quarters of the way through it. Plan for as long a time span as possible: a week, or a pay period, or, better yet, a month. We have a system we recommend. The beauty of using a method like *Once-a-Month Cooking* is expressed by one mom: " 'The time I'm not cooking every night frees me to pay attention to little things like setting the table or fixing a special dessert. When I had to cook every night, it was all I could do to deal with the meal. There wasn't time for extra touches, which I really enjoy,' " she said. " 'Those special times with family and friends can get lost in busy lives, and I don't want to lose them.' "[2] A month or two-week dinner cycle can be used as is from the book, or the method can be adapted to family favorites.

With planning, we can succeed more often in sandwiching a healthful family dinner between piano lessons and computer classes, between aerobics workouts and scout meetings.

▼ Stay Flexible ▼

Devise a plan and then reassess and modify it as family needs change. A spouse may shift to coming home midday for lunch or may begin traveling. You may start taking classes or go back to work. A child may develop allergies. Kids grow and change from picking at food to consuming it in large quantities. Adapt to the changes, incorporating them into your meal plan. The basics do not change, and your planning time is well spent.

▼ Planning Nuts and Bolts ▼

Study a calendar that plots the family's activities. Note the most promising times for your family to eat together, as well as those times when no one will be eating at home, times you will have company, times when kids will eat at home without parents, and vice versa. Make a note of times when dinner must be served early because of a meeting or a class or served late for any reason. On nights when the family will eat in shifts, a slow-cooker meal will be a lifesaver. Note on the calendar that you'll need to start the meal in the morning.

Now match menus to mealtimes, jotting on the calender what you'll serve each day.

Just for fun, try a new recipe each week. If it's a hit, attach it to an index card for your keeper file. If it's a dud, throw it away. If it's from a cookbook, write above the recipe the date you prepared it and the general reaction, so you'll know whether to bother with it again.

Plan meals with your family's likes and dislikes in mind—but once you've set the menu, try this rule:

Today's Menu
Two Choices:
Take It or Leave It

Keep a running shopping list on the refrigerator. Whenever your husband asks for chocolate ice cream or your daughter needs shampoo, ask them to write it on the list.

Every now and then you will serve—often by surprise—the perfect meal. Not only will each plate boast a pleasing variety of colors and food groups, but you'll

look around the table at empty plates and field requests for seconds. Write on an index card exactly what you served, and file it in a section labeled Menus.

Also keep menus you've used successfully for special occasions or for company. Keep a card, for example, on what you served this year for Thanksgiving dinner. Note dishes that won raves or dishes that did not go over well; note the number of people you served and any recipes that made too little or too much; write down what size turkey you cooked and how long you cooked it. Next Thanksgiving you can make some additions or deletions to the menu, but you won't have to start planning from scratch.

In the Menu section of your recipe file, keep track of menus that everyone likes and that you feel confident preparing for company. If you don't love to cook or have a particular flare for it, you can get a lot of mileage from one great company menu. The best menu is one that allows you to prepare much of it in advance.

Our friend Dawn keeps one menu she calls The Boss's Meal for an important guest dinner. But meals for company don't have to be gourmet. Who doesn't enjoy a meal prepared by someone else no matter what it is? It's more important that it be something the hostess (or host) feels comfortable preparing.

For fun, choose a food to become your specialty. For example, experiment with many kinds of soup, pancakes, homemade pizza, or stir-fry dishes. Become so proficient you can comfortably produce one of your specialities on short notice. It's fun to know you're good at something, even if it's quickly producing a colorful, fresh-looking salad.

Mimi's daughter Kyndra's specialty is baking bread, and she's made a rule for herself: She must always bake at least two loaves and then give one away.

Once you've developed your specialty, you can pull from your repertoire easy guest or take-to-others meals. Mimi has a friend whose specialty is pancakes with special toppings. Mimi's family ate a candlelight pancake breakfast in the warmth of this friend's home one cold Saturday morning, and it was as satisfying as any elaborate dinner—and more fun because of the novelty.

Gene, a single dad, tries to make dinnertime special for his three sons. He plans simple, solid meals: baked chicken; baked potato with sour cream; peas or corn or broccoli; pumpkin pie. The boys usually help start dinner before Gene gets home. One night a week is Choice Night, when each person can choose his dinner from whatever he finds on hand. But because Gene plans the meals, Choice Night is the exception, not the rule. Sunday nights the boys choose what they want Gene to fix for dinner, but they must agree on one menu.

One single, working mom capitalizes on weekend meals, which are much more manageable for her. Every weekend she and her children eat two meals together with a set table and candlelight. The kids love it and sometimes invite company for one of their special meals.

As an adjunct to careful planning, it is wise to keep on hand at least a few quick fixes for emergencies when the best laid plans fall through or are not enough. Following are some quick fixes you can supplement with your own ideas:

▾ **Baked potatoes** served for any meal can be stuffed with leftover cooked meat, cheese, sauce, or vegetables.

▾ **Leftover baked potatoes** may be fried for ▾**Margaret's Breakfast Burritos** or ▾**Country Fried Potatoes** (see recipes).

▼ **Pizzas** can be cooked, sliced, and frozen so the kids can pop a slice or two in the oven or microwave for a quick meal or snack.

▼ If you cook some dishes in quantities larger than you need for one meal, freeze the leftover amounts in **single portions** for lunch or for eating on the run.

▼ Whip up this easy **teriyaki sauce** for marinating chicken pieces, chunks of boneless chicken, or pork: ½ cup soy sauce, 1 tablespoon brown sugar, a pinch of ginger, and ½ teaspoon garlic powder.

▼ Keep a loaf of frozen French bread in the freezer and cans of some favorite **hearty soups.**

▼ In fact, always keep some **rolls** or **bread** in the freezer to stretch a meal.

▼ Keep a jar of **spaghetti** sauce, spaghetti and French bread.

▼ For a tasty, easy **chili**, keep on hand a jar of Tabasco brand chili, a pound of ground beef (frozen), a can of kidney beans, and a can of tomato juice. Try Fritos on your chili in place of soda crackers.

▼ Tuck in your freezer a recipe of ▼**Janet's Tortilla Hors d'Oeuvres** for drop-in guests.

▼ To perk up a snack, serve **apple** slices sprinkled with cinnamon and cheddar cheese wedges.

▼ **Tortillas** are so versatile! Warm them in the oven or microwave stuffed with cheese and salsa or leftover chili or leftover meat strips and rice or a casserole—endless combinations.

▼ **Rice** is versatile, too. Mix rice with a little Cajun seasoning and some grated cheese. Or serve rice with a can of warmed black beans and salsa.

▾ Keeping Within the Food Budget ▾

Careful menu planning will also help you shave money off your food costs. Beware of the two biggest budget busters: eating out frequently and dashing into the supermarket everyday. Eating in a restaurant costs roughly twice what it costs to prepare comparable food at home. Eating out is great for a family treat and American families are doing it more and more. But remember that it costs more, so make it a planned activity rather than a nothing-to-eat last resort. (We'll discuss family dining out in chapter 10.)

The problem with frequent grocery shopping is that it is next to impossible to enter and exit the grocery store without impulse buying. The layout of the store is designed to lure you to buy items you didn't know you needed. Buyers beware! The less often you set foot in the place, the more money you'll save. This is one beauty of the once-a-month cooking plan.

Here are some additional money-saving tips from Rhonda Barfield's book *Eat Well for $50 a Week*:

1. Set a limit on spending and stay under it with few exceptions.
2. Compare prices at nearby stores to see which store is least expensive overall.
3. Buy most groceries from the cheapest store.
4. Supplement by shopping at other stores whose weekly specials are outstanding.
5. Make a detailed shopping list and follow it to the letter, substituting only when unexpected bargains justify a change.[3]

One of the tragedies of big-city life is that for people living on a tight budget in the inner city, expensive convenience stores are more accessible than supermarkets.

Whenever possible, cook from scratch to save money. You pay for convenience in processing and packaging. Regular oatmeal costs a fraction of what you would pay for flavored instant oatmeal packets. Homemade bread costs a few cents, and its aroma is worth at least ten dollars. Weigh this in the time versus money debate: Our time is worth money, and we must keep assessing which is in shortest supply. Should I save money by cooking and deboning chicken, or save time by buying boneless chicken? Should I save money by preparing pancakes, or save time by serving cold cereal?

Survey the contents of the refrigerator and cupboards at least once a week. Often you'll find imaginative meal possibilities from items that need to be used up anyway. You'll cut down waste by not letting food spoil. One day I reached into the meat compartment for a package of turkey franks. Underneath it was a package of sirloin steak that was intended for a wonderful, but forgotten, meal. Then it was too brown and smelly for anything but guilt.

This little tip from home management specialist Bonnie McCullough has over the years saved me countless five o'clock trips to the grocery store: Each morning by 9:00 A.M., think through that evening's dinner so you'll have time to thaw food or prepare a gelatin salad, etc. If you must go to the store, at least you'll be able to plan when it best fits into your day.

Try to spend cash for groceries; it keeps you within your budget because when your cash is gone you have to stop buying. One woman keeps her grocery money in an envelope in the freezer (*cold cash*) so she knows where it is and is reminded not to spend it on other things. Using credit cards is risky business. It's a tragedy to pay interest on food.

Clip and use coupons, especially when stores are offering double value for coupons. If you don't have time to bother with coupons, enlist a child to clip and sort them. A child may require some supervision until he or she learns which coupons are really useful. You might even offer to pay the child half of what you save by using them, letting the child figure the arithmetic involved.

As you look through recipes you want to try, remember that in general the fewer the ingredients, the cheaper and easier the dish will be.

Investigate food co-ops available in your area and the possibilities of either swapping services for foodstuffs or for gleaning. Do you have a neighbor who would like some fruit trees gleaned in exchange for raking or fix-up work? Some areas have Share programs that offer a large quantity of food, including meat and produce, in exchange for a few hours of community service.

Exchange tips with a friend. Walk with a neighbor, find a friend through a group such as Mothers of Preschoolers (MOPS), visit with a coworker over lunch. Find someone who enriches your knowledge of those useful little things, like how to order window shades with an 800-number, where fresh blueberries have come down in price, who does good shoe repair, what great new recipe she has just tried.

No matter how much we have in our budget, the amount we spend on food usually comes down to a matter of wise or foolish use of our resources. How will we choose to use the resources God has enabled us to earn or receive? What are the wisest uses of our time as well as our money?

A warm meal can be an easy gift to give someone, with value lasting well beyond the time it takes to eat it. If giving of your time or money is extremely difficult, you may find that you can at least divide a dinner into five or six portions instead of four.

In downtown Quito, Mimi takes leftovers from the family's evening meal and arranges them on a paper plate. She adds a plastic fork and napkin, encloses the meal in a plastic bag, and sets it on the brick wall outside their home. A hungry person on the street at night won't have to go through the Wilson's trash for food, nor eat it with his hands. Instead of throwing away leftovers, she provides a meal and a sense of dignity.

It takes careful meal planning to keep family meals on keel and in line with what you have to spend. But it says you love your family members enough to want to plan for their physical and emotional health.

▾ Family Outing and Table Talk ▾

Some evening give each family member the same amount of cash (say, $4.00). Drive to an area with a number of fast-food restaurants clustered together. Let each go where he wants and purchase his own dinner, not to exceed the given amount of money. All meals should be carry out. Take them home and compare what each has been able to purchase.

Another evening give each family member $4.00 and go to the supermarket. Ask each to select and purchase his or her own dinner, minus dessert. Take all the items home and let each prepare his own. Discuss what the same money will buy at a fast-food restaurant versus in the grocery store. Compare the food value in the two types of meals.

Gingerbread Waffles

¼ cup sugar
2 tablespoons butter
2 tablespoons shortening
1 egg, well beaten
½ cup molasses
½ teaspoon ginger
¼ teaspoon cloves
1 ¼ cups sifted flour
¾ teaspoon soda
½ teaspoon cinnamon
⅛ teaspoon salt
½ cup hot water

Optional: *Whipped cream and fresh fruit*

Preheat waffle iron. Cream butter, shortening, and sugar. Add well-beaten egg and molasses. Stir together dry ingredients. Add to butter mixture. Add hot water and beat until smooth. Make waffles according to waffle iron instructions. Serve with maple syrup or whipped cream and fresh fruit. You may freeze the waffles and reheat in a toaster. Serves 4-5.

Tea at Ten
Ladyfingers
Decaffeinated herbal tea, with a patterned napkin tucked through the teacup handle for a little flair.

Table Talk:
Start a story. After a few sentences pass to the next person to add on and so around the table.

Saturday Breakfast
Gingerbread Waffles
Sausage (optional)
Cantaloupe and fresh grapes

Table Talk:
What would be your ideal vacation?

Family Dinner
Dawn Wilson's Boss's Meal
Raspberry Walnut Salad
▼ London Broil
▼ Crisscross Potatoes
▼ Butter Rolls
▼ Fresh Fruit Tart

Table Talk:
Which of your friends'
parents do you like/respect
the most and why?

Read from a list of state
capitals. Going around the
table, each person must
match the capital with
the state.

Slow-Cooker Dinner
Barbecued Beef
Sandwiches
Jell-O with fruit

Table Talk:
Give a sincere compliment
to the person on
your right.

Raspberry Walnut Salad

Dressing:
¼ cup vegetable oil
6 tablespoons sugar
4 tablespoons raspberry vinegar
2 tablespoons plain yogurt
2 teaspoons Dijon mustard
Salad:
6 cups leaf lettuce, washed, drained, chilled, and torn
½ cup walnuts, toasted* and coarsely chopped
½ cup fresh raspberries, washed and drained

Whisk together all dressing ingredients. Cover and refrigerate
for at least 1 hour. Place lettuce in a glass bowl; add walnuts.
Toss with dressing and raspberries. Serve immediately. Serves 6.
* To toast the nuts, spread in a single layer on a baking sheet.
Toast in a 300° oven until fragrant and golden, 20-25 minutes.
Shake sheet once or twice so they brown evenly.

Barbecued Beef Sandwiches

1 cup tomato juice
¼ cup Worcestershire sauce
1 tablespoon vinegar
1 teaspoon dry mustard
1 teaspoon chili powder
¼ teaspoon garlic powder

64

⅛ teaspoon ground cayenne pepper
1 2 ½- to 3-pound beef brisket or boneless beef chuck roast
8 hoagie buns, split

In a 2-cup measure combine juice, Worcestershire, vinegar, mustard, chili powder, garlic, and cayenne pepper.
　　Trim fat from meat. Place meat in a 3 ½- or 4-quart slow cooker, cutting as necessary to fit. Add juice mixture. Cover and cook on low-heat setting for 8 hours.
　　To serve, remove meat from cooker, reserving cooking juices. Slice thinly across grain. Skim fat from juices. Place meat in buns, spooning juices over the meat. Serves 8.

Chicken Fajitas

4 (8-inch) flour tortillas
1 pound boneless, skinless chicken breasts, cut into
*　finger-width strips*
1 teaspoon chili powder
½ teaspoon ground cumin
½ teaspoon pepper
¼ teaspoon salt
1 tablespoon lime juice
½ cup green onions, sliced
½ cup plain, nonfat yogurt
4 leaf-lettuce leaves
8 thin tomato slices, each cut in half crosswise

Quick and Easy
Chicken Fajitas and
Refried Beans
Cold Broccoli Salad
Sherbet

Table Talk:
Why are some people liked
and some are not?

Wrap tortillas in damp paper towels and then in aluminum foil. Bake at 350° for 7 minutes or until softened. Set aside.

Coat a large nonstick skillet with cooking spray; place over medium-high heat until hot. Add chicken, chili powder, and cumin; sauté 7 minutes or until chicken is not pink in center. Combine chicken, pepper, salt, and lime juice in a bowl and toss well. Add green onions and yogurt and toss well.

Place a lettuce leaf on each warm tortilla; divide chicken mixture evenly over lettuce. Top each tortilla with 4 tomato pieces; roll up. Serves 4.

Cold Broccoli Salad

Salad:
½ pound broccoli, cut into flowerets and small chunks (½-inch)
6 slices bacon, cooked crisp and crumbled
1 cup sunflower seeds or slivered almonds, toasted
1 cup raisins
Dressing:
¾ cup light mayonnaise
1 tablespoon raspberry vinegar
¼ cup sugar
Optional: *⅓ cup julienned canned beets, drained*

Toast the almonds on a pie plate for 20-25 minutes at 300° until lightly browned. Combine salad ingredients in medium-sized salad bowl. Stir together dressing ingredients and stir into salad. Refrigerate until serving. Serves 6.

▾ CHAPTER 5 ▾

TEAM-WORK

Children like to feel they can
accomplish tasks which contribute
to the life of the family.

It was Steve's night to wash dishes, and Steve did it differently from his four brothers, who just wanted to do it quickly and be done with it. Steve had his own style. First he set his buddy Sabrina, the little family dog, on the counter to keep him company. "Here, Sabrina, you hold the towel," he said as he draped the dish towel around Sabrina's neck. Then he plugged in his radio on the counter and turned to his favorite oldies station. As he scrubbed he sang, "Wake up, little Susie, wake up!" He took the towel from Sabrina, picked her up, and danced her around the kitchen. Steve figured he was going to be there a while and he might as well enjoy it.

Steve may be an exception to the rule, but most kids do see the need to help. Shared chores build a family team.

Mom doesn't have the time or energy to do all the work alone. The single parent or working mom, in particular, too often tries to do it all. But Mom's workload is not the point. All family members benefit from helping the household run smoothly, and they believe that they should. "In a survey of 250 children, over ninety-seven percent honestly felt they should work at home."[1]

Chores help children learn life skills and grow in self esteem. Children like to feel they can accomplish a task from start to finish and keep the home looking nice. They may not say so daily. They may grumble about a particular task or claim it's a sibling's turn to do it. But, in general, they like to help and know they should.

Unfortunately, the pace of parents and the needs of children often collide. Tired parents may find it easier or faster to do a job themselves. And if they expect the job done just so, perhaps they should do it instead of delegating it to a child.[2] But children like to feel accomplished and useful, and they should be given that privilege.

> Where no oxen are, the manger is clean,
> But much increase comes by the strength of the ox.
> —*Proverbs 14:4 (NAS)*

Dads, too, need to model teamwork and the willingness to serve. It helps if husbands and wives discuss household chores and their feelings about them. Some chores are important to a sense of masculinity or femininity, while others are neutral ground. Couples can divide the work as much as possible along the lines of the tasks each prefers, realizing there will be times when each will need additional help from the other.

If Mom is the primary meal manager, perhaps Dad will be the one to run errands on the way home from work. He may want to take on a particular weekend meal that becomes his domain.

Find a method of delegating chores and be consistent with it, like this one that works well in our family. On a large index card we divide chores (in this case meal-related chores) as equally as possible into three groups (for three sons). The groups may look like this:

Blue = Set table, assist cook
Yellow = Unload dishwasher, empty kitchen trash
Red = Wash pots and pans, put away food, wipe counters

The index card is taped to the bottom of the calendar that hangs in the kitchen. On the calendar in each Sunday square are marks of blue, yellow, and red. Beside each color is one of the boys' names. If Dan, for example, is blue one week, he will be yellow the next and red the following. Everyone knows that the jobs shift on Sunday and that if they don't like this set of tasks, at least they will change in a week. Everyone is responsible for bringing his own dishes from the table, rinsing them, and putting them into the dishwasher.

Children rarely balk at a task if they have a clear idea what is expected of them and when it must be completed. This involves patiently showing them how to do the task until they demonstrate they understand and can do it themselves. They need to know what equipment or cleaning supplies to use and where they are located. They need to know what performance standard is expected and when they need to finish the job.

The hard part for parents is ensuring that expectations are consistently maintained. If children are allowed to go two full weeks without doing their chores, they question whether they really need to do them at all. Inspect jobs when they are done. It says to a child that these tasks do matter. Be generous and genuine with compliments for a job well done.

When preschoolers are in the family, three- or four-year-olds can help, too. They can wipe tables and counters or wash vegetables. They can sort utensils and put them away or help set the table.

If children are old enough to be home before parents, they can help start dinner. "I leave directions on the refrigerator for whomever is home first," said a working mom. "As long as I've planned the meal and have given specific instructions, it goes really smoothly."

Chore time best becomes team-building time when it affords the chance to talk. The assistant cook position in our home is a natural for one-on-one time as we both stand at the stove to work. One mom in a rush to get a meal on the table will tell one of her kids, "Stick with me until we're finished, would you?" They talk as they work side by side.

Let kids express creativity in their tasks, giving them choices whenever possible: which place mats to use, which centerpiece, which dishes, and so forth. Avoid power struggles and yelling bouts over chores, which only frazzle you, hurt or anger the child, and serve no purpose.

> A gentle answer turns away wrath,
> But a harsh word stirs up anger.
>
> —*Proverbs 15:1 (NAS)*

Make requests without the tempting, cutting remark. Instead of saying "How many times do I have to tell you to take the garbage out after dinner?" say, "The trash is climbing the wall. It needs to go out now." Instead of saying "Jan, it's your turn to clean up and you're lying around watching TV," say "Clean up comes first, Jan. Then you can watch TV if your homework is finished." We all respond more positively when we are addressed in a tone of appreciation and respect.

Children are more eager to please and help at ages three, four, or five than they are at nine, ten or eleven. If there is a serious problem, withdraw a privilege, but don't nag. Hang onto your sense of humor.

Children seem more at peace with themselves, and with the rest of the family, when they understand and complete the tasks expected of them. A team effort at mealtime benefits the entire family.

Mealtimes are great levelers. The rich and the poor, the single and the large family, all deal with meals and associated chores every day. We all have to eat. And most of us don't like to eat alone. We can shape and do with those mealtimes what we wish.

Christian recording artist Twila Paris gives this preface to the song "The Joy of the Lord": "This past year has brought a new realization that the joy of the Lord is truly something very separate from my circumstances. Like many of the songs on this album, 'The Joy of the Lord' began as a spontaneous chorus that I would sing while washing dishes. (No wonder it takes so long to clean the kitchen!)"[3] Twila Paris not only eats dinner with her family, she washes the dishes, and composes music while she does.

At times we all get tired of the routine, but helping with mealtime builds a family team.

Cheese Bread

1 cup warm milk
½ cup warm water
1 package active dry yeast
¼ cup sugar
2 teaspoons salt
1 teaspoon dried dill weed
1 tablespoon minced onion
1 cup sharp cheddar cheese, grated
4 cups flour
Parmesan cheese
1 tablespoon melted butter

Dissolve the yeast in the warm milk and warm water. Let stand for 5 minutes. Add sugar, salt, dill weed, minced onion, and cheddar cheese. Add 4 cups flour, or enough so that the dough is no longer sticky. Knead with dough hooks or by hand about 5 minutes.

Let rise in greased bowl in a warm place 1 hour. Use ⅔ of the dough to form a loaf in a bread pan sprayed with nonstick spray. Form 3-inch round dinner rolls from the remaining dough and put on a baking sheet. Brush the tops with melted butter. Sprinkle with Parmesan cheese. Let rise another 40-60 minutes.

Bake bread at 350° for 30 minutes; bake rolls for 25 minutes. Cover lightly with foil if browning too quickly. Good with clam chowder or vegetable soup.

Tea at Ten
Cheese Bread
Decaffeinated herbal tea

Table Talk:
What worries you the most? Of what are you proudest?

Breakfast
▼ Country Fried Potatoes
Orange juice

Table Talk:
What is one new thing you would like to try?

73

Family Dinner
▼ Chili Mac
Tossed green salad
Easy Fruit Dessert

Table Talk:
Which chores around the house do you enjoy, and which do you dread?

Family Dinner
Grilled Marinated Flank Steak
▼ Corn on the Grill
Baked potato
Tomato slices
Jell-O Cake

Table Talk:
What was the funniest thing that happened to you today?

Easy Fruit Dessert

1 cup seedless red grapes
1 cup seedless green grapes
1 11-ounce can mandarin oranges or 1 fresh
  navel orange, sectioned
1 12-ounce can ginger ale
1 pint sherbet

Chill 4 dessert cups. Fill them with fruit mixture. Pour ¼ of chilled ginger ale over each serving. Top with 1 scoop of your favorite sherbet. Serve at once. Serves 4.

Grilled Marinated Flank Steak

Juice of 1 lemon
½ cup soy sauce
¼ cup red wine vinegar
3 tablespoons vegetable oil
2 tablespoons Worcestershire sauce
1 large clove garlic, sliced (or equivalent minced prepared garlic)
Pepper to taste
3 chopped green onions
1 teaspoon dried dill weed
1 ½-2-pound flank steak

Combine all ingredients and pour into a lock top bag. Marinate the flank steak in the bag which has been placed in a pan. Put pan in the refrigerator and turn the bag over occasionally for

2-12 hours. Broil meat over hot coals for 5 minutes per side for rare meat. Slice meat on the diagonal across grain. Serves 6.

Good with baked potato, vegetable, salad, and hot bread.

Jell-O Cake

1 3-ounce package gelatin, any flavor
1 cup boiling water
1 package white cake mix ("light" or regular)
¼ cup flour
¾ cup vegetable oil
4 eggs or egg substitute
Optional: sherbet—same flavor as gelatin

Dissolve the gelatin in the boiling water, stirring about 30 seconds. Cool slightly. Combine all ingredients except sherbet and beat at medium speed 4 minutes. Bake in greased and floured 9-inch tube pan at 375° for 40-45 minutes. Cool in pan 8-10 minutes. Remove from pan. Spoon glaze over warm cake (optional).

Glaze:
1 cup powdered sugar
1 tablespoon lemon juice

Mix sugar and lemon juice until smooth. Serve with same flavor sherbet as Jell-O. For Christmas, use cherry Jell-O and add a few drops of red food coloring. Frost with red-tinted icing and add cinnamon candies or pieces of maraschino cherry on top.

Family Dinner
▼ South of the Border
Casserole
Hawaiian Fruit Salad
Ice cream

Table Talk:
Children: What sort of work would you like to do when you grow up?
Adults: When you were a child, what did you want to do when you grew up?

Hawaiian Fruit Salad

2 3-ounce packages tapioca pudding
1 20-ounce can pineapple chunks (reserve liquid)
2 11-ounce cans mandarin orange sections
2 bananas, sliced
Optional: *1 6-ounce jar maraschino cherries*

Bring the pudding and 3 cups liquid from pineapple and oranges
(if necessary add water or orange juice to make 3 cups) to a boil
in a medium saucepan. Stir and cool. Add fruit. Refrigerate for at
least 6 hours. Stir in 2 bananas before serving. Garnish with
maraschino cherries for color. Serves 8.

CHAPTER 6

CELEBRATION OCCASIONS

Rituals are a family banner,
an expression of collective
personality and spirit.

I t's the first day of school, although it feels like any other late summer day; the sunshine through Hannah's bedroom window is already uncomfortably warm. Soon the yellow buses will roll, but first Hannah is enjoying breakfast in bed. On the wooden tray across her little lap is a plate of blueberry pancakes, melon balls, and a small cup of orange juice. She won't be a lady of leisure every day, but today is the first day of school and her mommy's mommy served her children breakfast in bed that day, so Hannah's mother does, too.

Family rituals unify and define the family. They are a family's pennant or banner, an expression of collective personality and spirit. "Through rituals, families create memories, continuity and a sense of being special, which in turn contribute to an individual's sense of self-esteem. Over time, as family members may develop different work, play and meal routines, traditions and rituals are especially valuable as they beat a steady rhythm behind unpredictable schedules."[1]

Family traditions are for Christmas, birthdays, graduations, and Easter, although some of the most distinctive traditions might spring up on April Fool's Day or the first day of spring. Anything your family "always does" is a family ritual.

Do you always eat pizza on Friday nights? That fits. One grandfather we know makes the rounds to his grandchildren's homes every Saturday morning to drop off doughnuts. Traditions are too significant as underpinnings to save only for major occasions.

As we present a collage of family traditions we have observed, we hope two things will happen. We hope you'll find a few that seem like a good fit for your family. More important, we hope you will realize and appreciate the wealth of rituals living in your own family, some of which you may have not yet identified.

One day Alex brought home from a construction site two finds that have since shown much greater potential than I ever thought they would. One was a hard hat that has served for backyard play, work projects, and Halloween costumes. The other was a many-yard-long string of plastic multicolor flags like those at used car lots. Since then, those flags—strung from the front of our house to trees and fenceposts—regularly symbolize that we're celebrating a family birthday. So does a photograph—posted on our front door—of the birthday boy as an infant or toddler.

The Wilson children celebrated their birthdays with a dinner that they planned and to which they invited the adults most special to them: a Sunday school teacher, coach, baby-sitter, and so forth. The guest list could include as many as 12, including immediate family members. The birthday child called and invited his guests. Within a set budget, he planned the menu and where they would eat (in the dining room, by the fireplace, in the backyard). He helped prepare the food, set and decorated the table, greeted the guests at the door, and took their coats. Before the event, Mimi discussed with him the fact that the guests might not all know one another, and suggested some topics of conversation that might include everyone. After opening each gift, the child thanked the giver, and sent a thank-you note after the party.

One time their son Kevin decided to treat his guests to Casa Bonita, an elaborate Mexican restaurant, complete with cliff divers and strolling singers. He carefully figured what it would cost, but when he came up short at the buffet line, he politely asked his guests not to order anything to drink.

Saturday breakfast for one family is time to build their own omelets. Arrayed on the counter are bowls of bits of the week's leftovers: sprouts, chives, green onion, taco meat, finely-cut roast beef, avocados, tomatoes, cheese, potatoes, etc. Mom whips up the omelets while each person chooses his or her own fillings.

A single mother and her four children are avid football fans. The mom prepares dips and special snacks or a meal for them to eat at halftime. Mom chooses not to invite friends over or accept any invitations during football games. The kids know she saves this time for their fun together.

Christmas in Ecuador is a time for the Wilsons to celebrate with neighbors and friends. Children carol from door to door at Christmas, and it is traditional to give each child a small gift.

Cal and Mimi and another couple hold a Scrooge Party. They include on their guest list people who don't seem to be invited out very often: large families, for example. The meal is casual, often a baked potato bar and, of course, Christmas goodies. They gather in the living room in front of the fireplace and watch the movie version of *A Christmas Carol*, starring George C. Scott. As Cal says, "It is a visible reminder to us of the wise retort given to Ebenezer Scrooge by the enchained ghost of his old partner, 'Mankind is our business!' "

Kurt Wilson is now married and lives in the States. When Kurt and Lori can't travel to Ecuador for Christmas, Mimi sends them some of her special holiday recipes with this note: "If I can't be preparing these for you here, I want at least to imagine you are enjoying them there."

Our own Christmas dinner centers around traditional Swedish lutefisk, which is a fish and rice pudding the Lagerborg family smothers in black pepper to

give it some flavor. It has become tradition that Alex's brother prepares the lutefisk, and it's tradition that while we eat it we compare it with last year's batch, and the best ever batch, and the batches that Grandma Lagerborg (the all-time standard) used to prepare. Unfortunately, most of the younger generation of Lagerborgs don't care for the stuff, but that is irrelevant. In fact, it seems even more important to keep serving it on Christmas as the generations pass away who relished it and felt a connection with their Swedish heritage.

Caroling parties also have become a favorite tradition. When our children were young we just invited adults to stroll around on a cold December night. Now that the children are older, we invite families. We ask each family to bring a flashlight.

We carol in our neighborhood, surprising neighbors because it's so seldom done any more. It's a genuine pleasure to share the joy of the season throughout the neighborhood.

Behind our caroling party is another motive: As we rehearse carols around the piano before we go out—using the same green song sheets each year—our children learn the majestic, old carols. They don't learn them in public school as we did, nor do they sing them enough in church to learn them from memory.

The night we decorate our tree, the youngest puts the angel on top, and we drink eggnog and eat Christmas cookies while we work. During the Christmas season we hold an extended family games, cookie bake, and craft night. The planned activities present a nice change of pace for a family that is frequently together, and through them we have discovered new things about each other.

Collect Christmas books and stories (check the sales after Christmas), and read aloud classics like *The Little Match Girl*, *The Gift of the Magi*, or *The Greatest Christmas Pageant Ever*. You can repeat them year after year.

For many years, we've celebrated New Year's Eve with a family of friends who have children our boys' ages. Our two families pool all our Christmas leftovers so we can wipe them out over the long evening and begin the New Year with a leaner régime. We play board games, watch movies, and cheer in the New Year. Now that our friends have moved to the mountains, we also spend the night at their home and end our celebration with a New Year's Day brunch. That particular tradition has weathered divorce and remarriage in the other family, although it meant the ritual was on awkward footing for a few years.

Mimi bakes a special Spring Cake (actually a chocolate cake, but any flavor would do) on the day that a family member spies the first sign of spring: a first hyacinth, for example, standing regal in the snow.

When fresh strawberries first hit grocery stores, Dawn Wilson serves strawberry shortcake at dinner because her mother used to do it when Dawn was growing up on a farm in Illinois.

And on April Fool's Day she serves a backward dinner. First comes an elaborate hot fudge sundae, followed by spaghetti and garlic bread, finishing with artichokes for dessert. To keep the family off guard, one year she served pizza for breakfast and scrambled eggs for dinner.

At Easter, Dawn's family lights their home with flashlights and candlelight from Good Friday until Easter morning. On Saturday night they read the Easter story from the Bible by lantern light. They talk about the darkness that settled over the world when Jesus died and the darkness that pervades the lives of those who don't yet know Him as Savior.

One Easter dinner at the Wilson's, Mimi asked a friend to hand-letter special place cards for each person at the table. On each card was the person's name, an Old Testament prophecy related to Easter, and a New Testament fulfillment of prophecy. The guests had to match their Old Testament prophecy with another guest's New Testament fulfillment. (See Table Talk at the end of this chapter.) The same thing can be done at a Christmas dinner.

Instead of going out for their anniversary, one couple eats a candlelight dinner at home that their children plan, prepare, and serve. The children are learning about romance and servanthood, as well as developing skills in the kitchen.

When all the cousins in one family were together, they baked, decorated, and consumed their own "cousins cake." The end of school for any grade, from preschool up, is another good excuse for a cake and a celebration of learning and accomplishments.

A trait of a healthy family, according to Dolores Curran, is that they have a strong sense of family in which rituals and traditions abound.[2]

Traditions give children memories to savor when they are grown up and far away. Because of the trials and hurts we endure in life, not every holiday or celebration will be a happy time for every family member. But over time, family rituals build strength and hope.

The person who has grown up with distinct family rituals is more likely to be resilient as an adult. "In a study of 240 college students and 70 of their parents, the more meaningful they felt their family rituals to be, the more positive was the

students' sense of themselves, and the better able they were to bear up under stresses of the freshman year."[3]

When we decorate our Christmas tree this year I will let the boys—if they want to—sleep near the tree in sleeping bags that first night. Now 12 years old, our youngest may be the last holdout to want to do it. But if he still wants to, he'll never be too old. We must not make the mistake of ending a tradition prematurely, assuming our children are too old to be interested. They may still enjoy or depend on the security a ritual affords them.

As Alex Haley said, "The family is our refuge and springboard; nourished on it, we can advance to new horizons. In every conceivable manner, the family is link to our past, bridge to our future."[4]

Sour Cream Gingerbread

2 eggs
½ cup sour cream
½ cup molasses
½ cup brown sugar
1 ½ cups flour
1 teaspoon baking soda
1 teaspoon ginger
¼ teaspoon salt
½ cup melted butter or margarine
Optional: *Whipping cream, whipped topping, or applesauce*

Preheat oven to 350°. Spray an 8- or 9-inch square or heart-shaped pan with nonstick spray. Beat eggs. Add sour cream, molasses, and brown sugar and beat again until smooth. Sift in dry ingredients. Beat again and when all the lumps are gone, stir in melted butter. Spread in the pan and bake 25 minutes. Serve warm or cool, with whipped cream, whipped topping, or applesauce. Serves 8-10.

Tea at Ten
Christmas cookies
Eggnog

Table Talk:
Read a few favorite Christmas carols as if they were poetry. Discuss the significance of the lyrics.

Birthday Breakfast in Bed
Sour Cream Gingerbread
An orange half with a candle in it (if an adult will be in the room!)

Table Talk:
Talk about fond memories of the birthday person, including the pregnancy with the child and her birth. Discuss which family members she resembles most in looks and temperament.

Easter Dinner

Chicken Florentine
▼ Sweet-and-Sour Tossed
Salad
Dinner rolls
▼ Lemon Cake

Table Talk:

On each place card print
an Old Testament
prophecy relating to
Easter and a New
Testament fulfillment.
Scramble them so that one
person's card has the
prophecy and another
person's the fulfillment.
Then each person must
find the match.

Old Testament prophecies
and New Testament
fulfillments:

Isaiah 50:6 . . . Mark 15:9
Isaiah 53:8 . . . Mark 14:54
Isaiah 53:9 . . . Mark 15:46
Zech. 13:6 . . . Mark 15:24
Psalm 22:1 . . . Mark 15:34

Chicken Florentine

1 10-ounce package frozen, chopped spinach
2 tablespoons butter
2 tablespoons flour
2 cups milk
Salt and pepper
⅛ teaspoon nutmeg
1 tablespoon butter
1 tablespoon olive oil
6 boneless, skinless chicken breast halves
Paprika
½ pound sliced fresh mushrooms
1 cup shredded mozzarella cheese
¼ cup grated Parmesan cheese

In a nonstick skillet, cook the frozen spinach over medium heat
until defrosted. The cooking will remove some of the liquid, but
drain the spinach in a colander, pressing the remaining liquid
out with a large spoon.

Make a white sauce by melting 2 tablespoons butter in
a saucepan, stirring in the flour, then the milk. Heat on medium
high, stirring constantly, until the sauce boils and thickens.
Season with salt, pepper, and nutmeg.

Add the spinach to the white sauce, and pour into a
9x13x2-inch baking dish treated with nonstick spray. Wipe out
the skillet with a paper towel. Cut the chicken into bite-sized
pieces and sauté them in the 1 tablespoon butter and olive oil in
the skillet until no longer pink in the center. Season chicken

with salt, pepper, and paprika. Spoon chicken on top of
the spinach.

In the same skillet, now sauté the mushrooms in remaining
drippings. Put the mushrooms on top of the chicken, then
sprinkle the mozzarella and Parmesan cheese over the top.
Refrigerate at this point if you are preparing the dish ahead.
(Can be refrigerated a day ahead, or the dish may be frozen.)
Bake at 350° for 30-40 minutes or until bubbly. Serves 6-8.

Red Beans and Rice

1 cup dried red kidney beans, red beans, or black beans
4 cups water
1 cup onion, chopped
½ cup green pepper, chopped
½ cup green onion, chopped
2 bay leaves
½ teaspoon thyme
2 cloves garlic, minced
¼ teaspoon ground black pepper
6 ounces turkey ham cut into ½ inch cubes
1 teaspoon salt
2 cups hot cooked natural long-grain brown rice, no salt
  or fat added
Optional: Sour cream, salsa, and/or chopped green onions

Isaiah 53:12 . . .Mark 15:27
Zech. 9:9 . . . Luke 19:30
Isaiah 53:7 . . . Mark 15:3
Psalm 22:18 . . . Luke 23:34

Family Dinner
Red Beans and Rice
Baked squash
Corn bread
Brownies

Table Talk:
Research your family
heritage(s) and discuss.
Find some old family
recipes or recipes
traditional to your ethnic
heritage(s) to try at future
family dinners.

Table Talk:
When you are gathered
with grandparents, ask
them to tell about any
particularly colorful
characters they remember
from the family line.

Rinse the beans under cold water and soak covered with cold water overnight. Drain. Simmer all ingredients *except* the rice, salsa, sour cream, and green onions in a large covered saucepan for 1 ½ hours, or until the beans are tender and the sauce is thick. The mixture can simmer in a slow cooker on low heat for 8 hours.

If you want fairly firm beans but a thick gravy at the same time, mash ½ cup of the cooked beans and stir back into the pot. This will thicken the remaining liquid. Spoon ½ cup of rice onto each plate and ladle the red bean mixture over or around the rice. Serve with salsa or a dollop of sour cream and chopped green onions. Serves 4.

Sloppy Joes

1 ½ pounds ground beef
1 10 ¾-ounce can chicken gumbo soup
¾ cup ketchup
⅓ cup brown sugar
8 hamburger buns

Brown meat in skillet. Drain fat, add soup, and stir. Add catsup and brown sugar. Stir well. Bring to a boil, then simmer covered for 15 minutes. Serve on hamburger buns. Serves 8.

Springtime Family Dinner
Sloppy Joes
Tater tots or French fries
Broccoli
Whole fresh strawberries: dip in sour cream, then in brown sugar

Table Talk:
What is your favorite family tradition?

CHAPTER 7

SETTING EXTRA PLACES

A warm meal and warm conversation are great yet simple gifts.

When Mimi was a child, her parents and grandparents were missionaries to the Pygmies in the Ituri Forest of what was then the Belgian Congo, now Zaire. The nearest grocery store, as Mimi puts it, was two countries away. Yet their home was known for the warm hospitality of her mother, Ella Spees. The few travelers along the rutted jungle roads knew they would find there a meal and place to stay through the black jungle night. Their home was even listed in a European travel guide.

Mimi remembers once waking up to find herself sleeping in the bathtub because her bed was needed for guests who had come in the night. As usual, the plug was in the drain to keep out the snakes. Her mother said with a twinkle in her eye, "Heidi gets to sleep in the attic, and you get to sleep in the tub." She made it all seem fun.

When Calvin and Mimi were married, they intended to open their home to others as Mimi had seen her mother do. But Mimi had attended boarding school and had done very little cooking, so she had a rugged start.

Immediately after their honeymoon, Mimi invited Cal's parents as their first dinner guests. They were living in a mobile home while Cal attended medical school. Their budget was spare, so Mimi decided to specialize in homemade soups. She tried chicken soup for the first time that night for Don and Chris Wilson. The recipe, her own, consisted of a canning kettle full of water, a chicken, a handful of rice, a handful of cherry tomatoes, an onion, and several bay leaves because she liked their shape. As Mimi says, it was not even colored water. At the end of the meal Don pushed back his chair and said to his wife, "Chris, you must get Mimi's recipe!"

In the many years and meals since, Mimi has seen time and again a lesson she learned as a child. Hospitality is a ministry; the family gives and it also receives.

Hospitality is commanded in the Scripture: "Be hospitable to one another without complaint."[1] Why? God may want to work in the lives of the host, or the guest, or both, as in the stories of Abraham entertaining strangers who were angels, and the widow who made bread for Elijah with her last bit of flour and oil.[2]

God wants us to hold all we have without grasping. An effective way to communicate God's love is to gently, practically attend to the needs of others. Hospitality (from the same root as *hospital*) is seeing needs in others and reaching out to meet them, even if it's merely with a warm meal or place to stay for the night.

A family must feel secure in itself before it can open its home to guests. And the family must keep a healthy balance between company and just-family times. If we don't maintain vitality within our family, we don't have much to share with others. On the other hand, if we keep all that family warmth to ourselves, others miss out and we do, too.

Entertaining guests doesn't have to throw the family, especially the mom, into turmoil. As Rachael Crabb says in *The Personal Touch*, "Hospitality is encouragement. Keep it simple. Keep it your style."[3]

How can your family encourage others? What is your style? Think in terms of what you have to offer, not in terms of what you don't—a fireplace, a big shade tree, a patio, a great coffee cake recipe. It's not the decor or even the menu that's important. You will always be in homes nicer than your own, as well as ones not so nice. If you can invite a friend to your home when it isn't immaculate, it frees her to reciprocate. She thinks, *If her home looks like this, I think I could have her over to my house.*

Concentrate on cleaning the rooms guests will really use: the living or family room, a bathroom, the kitchen, a bedroom if it's an overnight stay. If they wander down into a basement storage room or walk into your teenager's bedroom . . . oh, well!

What is your style of cooking? Casual, gourmet, or somewhere in between? Don't hesitate to ask a guest to bring a dish; guests usually feel better if they are able to contribute somehow. If you enjoy spending the day preparing a gourmet meal, go for it. What's important is the welcome: treating guests like family, and family like guests.

▾ Who Needs A Dose ▾ Of What You Have To Give?

Who in your sphere of influence would benefit from what your family has to give? Do you have older neighbors or friends? If you don't have grandparents living nearby, consider adopting some. Invite them to your children's band concerts, the Scout courts of honor, or any night for dinner. They will love the family activity even if you serve them macaroni and cheese. So they can fully enjoy a meal with you, be aware of any dietary restrictions they might have. If your guest is a good storyteller, prime him or her by asking leading questions.

Mimi's family has adopted an elderly neighbor in Quito, a lonely woman named Maruja. She will sit and watch Mimi and her family for hours, not demanding any attention. One day as Mimi got into the car to drive to the market, Maruja

climbed in the passenger side. "Do you know where we're going?" Mimi asked. "What does it matter?" Maruja replied. Many times with older people it doesn't matter what you are doing. They just love to be included.

Do you know some young singles? Let them help you prepare dinner or get them involved with the kids in a basketball game.

Single-parent families usually find themselves with fewer family invitations during a time in their lives when they need and want more. A warm meal and conversation, and the chance for kids to play with other children, is a great gift. Occasionally we invite a single dad and his sons on a Sunday afternoon to watch football and eat a bowl of chili, buffet style. Guess who is first in line at the buffet, with a wide grin? The dad, who hasn't been cooked for in a long time.

When we were newlyweds, Alex and I lived in a tiny house on a large, wooded lot in a college town. Every Sunday evening a group of college girls came to our house for Bible study and just to get away from the dorm. To them it seemed a world away from campus life. Since we were on a tight budget, we learned to be inventive with snacks. Popcorn goes a long way, and those holiday boxes of assorted cheeses, sausages, and crackers could feed several of us for lunch. An older couple helped us by bringing over sodas and food (a simple but appreciated gift).

Are there families that you would like to see more often? Cal and Mimi and another family get together on Friday nights for what they call "being tired together." They build a fire in the fireplace and watch a videotaped movie. They pool leftovers for dinner or order pizza, and the younger children arrive already dressed in their pajamas. Sometimes the best times are the most casual.

George and Barbara Bush entertained more guests, including house-guests, in the White House than any other presidential family. A picture in a newspaper showed the President and First Lady sitting in bed on a Saturday morning with a gaggle of grandchildren around them. How refreshing to see a First Family share that magnificent, big White House.

On nights when you would like to have good just-adult conversation, six adults seems to be a good number. If your guests don't know each other, serve something unusual like fondue, which forces guests to sit closer and to interact with each other.

Some of our favorite guests have been Alex's friends traveling through town on business, who would rather spend a night with a family than stay in yet another hotel. They're able to relax and feel closer to their own homes and families.

We need to try to assess our guests' needs. Sometimes a big meal is not what is needed for company. One time a friend stayed in our home en route from Pennsylvania to California. He suffered from chronic back trouble, and by the time he drove into Denver he was stiff and hurting. It was obvious that he didn't need to sit down to a major meal. What he enjoyed that night was something light to eat followed by a rousing game of tennis under the lights.

▼ Children Give In Ways We Can't ▼

Young children and company can be a precarious mix because we're never quite sure how the children will behave. On the other hand, children can touch a chord in a person in ways no adult can. Mimi knew a young man who came to their

home after being released from prison. His family had deserted him, and the man was despondent and alone.

Kevin, who was about four, walked up to the stranger sitting in his living room. "Mister, is that your car outside?" Kevin asked.

"Yes, it is," he said.

"Well, it sure is a neat one," he said, as he crawled into the man's lap. Tears rolled down the man's face. Mimi could not hold this emotionally starved man, but Kevin could.

In many households the kids wait in front if they know company's on the way. Wouldn't you like a welcome like that? At Dawn's house a frequent guest, a young single man, is wrestled to the floor by Dawn's children as soon as he enters the door. When they've all had enough of that, the fellow lifts six-year-old Hans to his shoulders and walks to a canister on a high shelf where Dawn keeps packets of seaweed, a gift from Japanese guests. Hans removes a packet and he and the guest chew on the seaweed. It's their routine.

Dawn also keeps books of interest to all ages. One of these is Stephen Biesty's *Incredible Cross Sections*, which shows in marvelous detail cross sections of a castle and a train and all sorts of other things. Her children have learned, on their own, that anyone will be interested in seeing and talking about these books. A child brings a book to the living room, and a conversation begins.

▼ Hospitality to Go ▼

Many years ago a workman on a street crew gave three homemade tamales to Kurt Wilson, who was playing nearby. "Take these to your mother and tell her

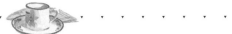

Jesus loves her," the workman said. When Mimi went outside to talk to the man he explained to her, "I just want to do something for people and tell them about Jesus, but all I know how to do is make tamales." So he made tamales and gave them away.

What do you have from your kitchen that you could give away to brighten someone's day? Can you wrap up a little lasagna for a shut-in for a friend who could use a special touch? Let the children help you prepare and take it.

When our son Tim was in the first grade, his teacher nearly died after complicated surgery. During her long recovery at home, Tim and a classmate took her dinner and ate with her by candlelight.

When Mimi knows friends are leaving Quito on a trip, she likes to take over warm brownies or juice and individual meat pies for them to take along. It's a way of sharing the joy, of saying "I'm happy for you."

Take food to a home where someone is ill or there has been a death in the family. Consider what foods will be appetizing if someone is ill. When a woman's husband died suddenly in an accident, neighbors rallied and brought over a platter of cold cuts, breads, mayonnaise, mustard, fresh fruit, cut-up vegetables, and paper products including tissues. During the following week they all stocked her freezer with precooked meals.

▼ Realistic Expectations ▼

Sure you will have a few disasters, but try to keep laughing and carry on. One night we were having a couple over for dinner and I was tired and trying to keep it simple. I should have known I had a problem when a good friend stopped

by—the kind of friend who tells you the truth—and when I told her what I was serving she said, "I'm not impressed."

At the end of the meal Alex looked across the table at me and asked, "Is that all there is?" The men went to Baskin-Robbins and brought home some ice cream.

On a rare occasion, a guest may prove difficult. When that happens, after the meal I like to take the tablecloth outside and shake it, look at the stars, and take a breath of fresh air. Find some way to keep your perspective as well as your composure.

If the meal is not ready as soon as you had hoped it would be, hand your guest a photo album or a book of excellent photography and ask her to make herself at home in the living room.

A guest is too talkative? Hold a quick family meeting and agree to take turns being the primary listener. Even in this situation, the children will learn skills that will carry over into adult life.

During a meal, seat yourself between your children. Don't make them the center of attention. After a meal with company, let the children go about their regular business—homework, bedtime, whatever—unless they want to be involved or their presence seems particularly important.

Do you get bogged down in the same conversations with people you see frequently? Plan a game or activity, use place cards to change the seating order, suggest everyone go for a walk, or lighten the time by including other guests.

As for the menu, don't try to be more elaborate than you can easily handle, and plan and prepare as much of the meal as possible ahead of time. Be flexible. Did the roast shrink too much? Make plenty of gravy, shred the meat and serve it on sandwich rolls. If you don't call attention to a problem, it probably won't be noticed.

▼ The Receiving End ▼

We would be hard pressed to know who receives the greater gift: the host family or the guests. Children can be the biggest winners. By seeing others treated with courtesy, and being courteously treated themselves, they learn that people have worth. Children learn to be sensitive to other people's feelings, and to participate easily in conversation with all ages. Children are enriched as they listen to people who sell real estate or work with heavy equipment, who design rocket components or overhaul bicycles. Often children become eager to invite over people they want to get to know.

Our son Tim went through several torturous treatments on a chronically ingrown toenail. The doctor who put him through the painful sessions was compassionate toward him. One day on our way home from the doctor's office, Tim said to me, "We should have her come for dinner." It was his highest compliment.

Two couples came to our home for dinner one night. The six adults sat down at the table. On this evening we had planned not to include the children. Our boys came and went quietly, sometimes watching TV in the next room. We adults sat in candlelight and began talking about gangs, guns in the hands of children, and the urban poor. One of the couples lived in a part of the city where all three problems were rampant. As our friend Ramiro spoke with anger, compassion, and conviction, one of our teenage sons quietly pulled up a chair. Another slipped in and sat on the floor. The older son ventured some comments, tentatively, as if testing his perceptions against what he was hearing. Mostly the boys listened—and learned.

Not only are children the receivers, we adults are too. Maruja, Mimi's neighbor who goes to the market with her, could not be a more loyal friend. In her eyes

Mimi can do no wrong. The college girls who came to our home in the woods made eager, caring baby-sitters. The traveling businessmen who visit our home have become like uncles to our sons.

One way a family receives is with a house that is alive with laughter. Homes up and down every street hold lonely people, but a house that knows company is a house that knows good cheer. Besides laughter, there will be energy to extend our hearts to people who are emotionally, if not physically, hungry.

> And if you give yourself to the hungry,
> And satisfy the desire of the afflicted,
> Then your light will rise in darkness,
> And your gloom will become like midday.
> And the Lord will continually guide you,
> And satisfy your desire in scorched places,
> And give strength to your bones;
> And you will be like a watered garden,
> And like a spring of water whose waters do not fail.
> —*Isaiah 58:10, 11 (NAS)*

Mimi's mother, who was so hospitable in the Belgian Congo, is suffering the advanced stages of Alzheimer's disease. She doesn't recognize Mimi when she visits her, but she graciously invites her in: "Come sit here by me, Dear. There's plenty to eat. Come talk to me." A graciousness remains, and no bitterness with it.

Mimi doesn't sleep in bathtubs these days, but their beds are usually full. She is developing care and treatment programs for disabled youths in Ecuador. Rosa, her househelper, is her partner. Rosa finds needy children through her connections in the barrios and brings them to Mimi's door. Rosa found one girl, Monica, in a bar. Monica has cerebral palsy and was hopelessly twisted and abused.

Mimi and Rosa put Monica in Mimi's bathtub and gave her her first tub bath. They put her in a clean nightgown and tucked her into clean sheets. Later they took her to a place where she receives loving care. It's the simple things that count. It's the welcome that matters. The family that gives it is twice blessed.

Fiesta Yogurt Breakfast

1 8-ounce carton low-fat vanilla yogurt
2 cups low-fat granola
1 ⅓ cups diced fresh fruit in season: blueberries, sliced peaches,
  pears, strawberries, or apples

In medium bowl, stir together yogurt and granola and fold in fruit. Divide into individual bowls. Serves 4.

*Ham and Green Bean Casserole

2 10 ¾-ounce cans cream of celery soup
1 cup milk
1 cup grated sharp cheddar cheese
½ cup grated Parmesan cheese
1 ½ teaspoons minced onion
1 tablespoon prepared mustard
1 tablespoon lemon juice
⅛ teaspoon rosemary leaves
½ teaspoon pepper
1 8-ounce package medium egg noodles, cooked
4 cups cubed, cooked ham
2 16-ounce cans French-style green beans, drained
1 6-ounce can French fried onions

Tea at Ten
Bagels and
Cream Cheese
Decaffeinated herbal
tea

Table Talk:
What do you think
about guardian angels?

Breakfast
Fiesta Yogurt
Breakfast
Toast
Fruit juice

Table Talk:
In what ways does TV
influence your life?

Dinner to Go
Ham and Green Bean
Casserole
Sliced kiwi, banana and
strawberries or other
fresh fruit medley
in season
Oatmeal Chocolate Chip
Cake

Table Talk:
Share an
embarrassing
experience.

Family Dinner
Shannon's Low-Fat
Chicken Rellenos
Refried beans
Ice cream with
▼ Chocolate Sauce

Warm and stir the celery soup and milk in saucepan or microwave it. Add next 7 ingredients and stir over low heat (or microwave it) until cheese melts.

Add the cooked noodles and ham to the soup mixture. Place ½ of soup mixture in 9x13-inch pan treated with nonstick spray. Pour the beans over the top, then the other half of the soup mixture. Bake 50 minutes at 350°. Ten minutes before it's done add French fried onions to the top and return to oven.
Serves 12.
*Used by the ladies of Mission Hills Baptist Church in Littleton, Colorado.

Oatmeal Chocolate Chip Cake

1 ¾ cups boiling water
1 cup quick-cooking or regular oatmeal
1 cup brown sugar
1 cup sugar
½ cup margarine
2 eggs
1 ¾ cups flour
1 teaspoon baking soda
½ teaspoon salt
1 tablespoon cocoa
1 12-ounce package chocolate chips
Optional: ¾ cup chopped pecans or walnuts

Pour boiling water over oatmeal in large mixing bowl. Let stand at room temperature 10 minutes. Add sugars and margarine. Mix on low speed until margarine melts. Add eggs. Mix on medium speed for 2 minutes. Add flour mixture. Add ½ of chocolate chips. Mix well with a spoon. Pour into floured and greased 9x13-inch pan. Sprinkle rest of chips and nuts on top. Bake at 350° for 40 minutes.

Table Talk:
Discuss salaries. Give four or five examples of average wages for different occupations. Do wages necessarily match the value or significance of the work done?

Family Dinner
▼ Easy Oven Lasagna
Tossed Green Salad
Hot French Bread

Table Talk:
What famous person would you like to have as a guest at the table? What would you talk about with that person?

Shannon's Low-Fat Chicken Relleños
(A dish to make ahead and freeze)

4 skinless, boneless chicken breasts
2 ounces low-fat Monterey Jack cheese, sliced
1 7-ounce can whole green chilies
½ cup cornmeal
1 egg white
2 tablespoons water
Optional: *Salsa*

Pound the chicken breasts until they are flat. Cut four green chilies in half and remove seeds. Place one green chili on each of the four chicken breasts. Insert ½-ounce slice of cheese inside each green chili. Roll up chicken breasts and secure with a toothpick. Dunk each in a bowl filled with the egg white and water then roll in cornmeal. Put each relleño in a separate lock-top bag in the freezer. To prepare for serving, remove from the freezer and thaw. Place thawed breasts on lightly greased cookie sheet and place in 350° oven for 45 minutes or until tops are lightly browned and cheese is oozing out the sides. Remove toothpicks and serve the chicken relleño over Spanish rice. Pass salsa if desired.

Spur-of-the-Moment Barbecue

You see friends at a summer sports event or outdoor concert and want to get together afterward. Have each person or family bring one of these items: Chicken pieces and a bottle of barbecue sauce, watermelon, corn on the cob and a stick of butter (margarine), French bread and a stick of butter (margarine), and ice cream with two toppings. You start the grill and provide iced tea, lemonade, decaffeinated coffee, and the table service. So easy it's fun for you, too.

▼ CHAPTER 8 ▼

THE WORLD AT YOUR TABLE

When international friends share
your table, your family can view the
world through their eyes.

W hat do the prime minister of the Czech Republic, the king of Nepal, and the prime minister of Pakistan have in common? Each of them was at one time a student in the United States.[1] I wonder what they thought of America and Americans? I wonder if they were invited into homes for dinner or for Thanksgiving?

After World War II, the United States opened its borders to students from all over the world with the hope of training future leaders of less-developed countries. Those men and women could then return to help their countries progress more rapidly.

Now there are in the U.S. more than 523,000 foreign students from almost 200 countries at any one time.[2] They represent their countries' brightest and most promising citizens. Many will become heads of state, cabinet members, university professors, newspaper editors, generals, business executives, ambassadors, lawyers, doctors, bank presidents, pastors, or seminary professors. In fact, "The majority of international visitors in the United States, including students, 'are destined in the next twenty-five years to occupy one-fourth to one-half of the world's top positions of leadership—politically, militarily, economically, scientifically, academically and socially.' "[3]

That's what they become later, when they are back in their homelands. Here in America they are likely to be lonely, insecure, homesick, and eager to make friends. Most international students would love to meet Americans and learn about their culture. But fewer than one-fourth of them are ever guests in an American home. What a tragedy for us all!

Can you imagine how bewildering America must be for a visitor from another culture? A Finnish friend, Anne, arrived in Chicago en route to her destination in Denver. Her flight was delayed and she had to call the people who would be waiting for her. Anne exchanged her money, but she did not know the worth of each U.S. coin. She stuffed coins into the pay phone continuously until her call was completed.

▾ Getting to Know You ▾

How do we meet international students? Most universities have a foreign-student adviser who would be happy to help. Often they have a host-family program. Host families don't usually house the student; they meet with him or her periodically to help smooth the way through our culture and to help them develop friendships. In many cities, International Students, Inc., (ISI) works with churches and foreign student advisers to match students with host families. ISI also has a program, Professionals in Partnership (PIP), that matches American professionals and businesspeople with internationals in the same fields of study— engineers with engineering students, doctors with premed students, and so on.[4]

Befriending international students is not necessarily time consuming. They don't need so much for us to do things for them as much as to do things *with* them. "They are, by and large, courteous, ambitious, bright and sociable."[5] Generally they are serious students and don't have much time to socialize. But it is a serious commitment. It takes openness, flexibility, and the determination to be consistent even if we do not see the student frequently. We must be willing to learn and to be patient with people groping with English-language skills.

In other cultures, people usually have a few close friends. Consequently, they can tell when Americans are not genuinely interested in them or when Americans have their own agenda. One international student gave this scathing commentary: "Americans are very friendly, but they don't make good friends."[6]

Once you meet one student, you can easily meet 50; they'll introduce you to other internationals. In fact, you might take the initiative to encourage a student to bring a friend to your home when she visits. It might make her feel more comfortable.

Once you have set a time to meet, follow up your telephone call with a written note confirming the date, time, place, and how they will get there. Include your family names, ages of your children, and pets' names, so they can orient themselves before they come. Pray that you will know how to give and receive friendship from one another.

What do you do with an international friend? An important first step is to learn to pronounce his or her name correctly. During our first meal with our Italian friend, Michael (pronounced Me-kay'-lay), he asked us earnestly, "Please try to say my name correctly. The other things aren't important, but this is my name." We practiced at home, correcting each other. The children learned it quickest.

The form of greeting is important in many cultures. What is considered proper; what is offensive? In Ecuador, people go around the room and touch right cheeks with each person, kissing into the air, even if they are late for a meeting that has begun. Don't hesitate to ask about such things if you don't know.

Take time to learn a bit about the student's country before he visits your home. When he comes, ask him to locate his country for you on a map. Ask him basic questions about physical features, climate, historic places, recreational areas, and his own home environment. What ethnic groups live there? What religions do they practice? What is their form of government? How large is his family? What work do his parents do?

Simple refreshments work well for a first visit: coffee, tea, or fruit juice and cookies or crackers. Remember that it is considered impolite in many cultures to accept them on the first or second offer. You may need to offer them several times.

During his first visit with you, arrange a second visit. That will help confirm your interest in him.

Ask to see photos of the student's family. Give him pictures of him with your family, in case he would like to mail them home.

Include your student in normal family activities. Invite him over for spaghetti or a family birthday party; take him shopping with you or to a basketball game. Invite him to accompany you to a wedding, a graduation, or some other special event. You might learn from and participate with him in his favorite activity. Generally, students like to work in the kitchen and learn to prepare American food. If so, teach him how to cook a hamburger or prepare a Thanksgiving turkey. Mostly they just like to feel welcome in an American home.

In Ecuador, Mimi and her family were invited to dinner at the home of Rosa, her househelper. The occasion was Kyndra's departure to the States for college. Rosa borrowed chairs from a furniture store for the event. She soaked the vegetables in chlorine and water (as she would do in the Wilson home but not in her own).

She printed a banner—God bless you in travel—and hung it on the wall. The welcome was overwhelming as Rosa's neighbors stood in their doorways to greet them. Internationals are not likely to feel so welcome in the U.S. "In a study published in 1976, 40 percent of the 247 foreign students surveyed at 38 Southern universities felt 'unwelcome, lonely, and isolated,' and the situation is not much different in the North."[7]

Use jokes and humor sparingly around your new friend. Your guest probably won't understand the humor and may feel left out or, worse, that the laughter is at his or her expense. If you say something which from your friend's expression you can tell was obviously inappropriate, simply apologize and talk about something else. Since older people are revered in many cultures, an older parent or other relative may contribute a great deal in helping a student feel at home. Playful children help as well.

When Xiong, a Chinese graduate student, first visited Aaron and Joan in their home, neither he nor they knew how significant their connection would be. Xiong had had to leave his wife and daughter in China, and he missed them tremendously. Aaron and Joan's two daughters reminded him of his own child, and it meant much to him to spend time with them.

If a spouse and children accompany a student to the U.S., they may be particularly isolated and need friends since they will not have the day-to-day interactions with teachers and other students on campus.

▼ Mingling Cultures at the Table ▼

Invite an international friend to cook in your kitchen a favorite meal from her culture. Better yet, ask her to teach you to prepare her favorite dish. Offer to supply the food or take her shopping. If she lives in a dorm, she has no opportunity to cook and will miss preparing her own foods. Students enjoy being able to share their culture.

Always ask if your new friend observes any dietary restrictions: Hindus and Buddhists generally don't eat beef, and Muslims and most Jews don't eat pork.

Keep the meal and table settings simple. Did you know that half the world's population eat with their hands, a fourth use chopsticks, and only a fourth use silverware?[8] Many international students prefer simple fruit desserts or ice cream to rich, heavy sweets.

If you have the opportunity to meet people from a number of cultures, hold a potluck dinner and ask each guest to bring a favorite dish from his or her country, labeling what it is and where it is from.

Not every cross-cultural experience will be with students. You may meet internationals through your church or business. A friend from church hosted three members of the African Children's Choir while they were in town. For dinner she served hamburgers, French fries, sodas, and a birthday cake for one of the choir members. The birthday cake was a novelty and went over big. Their next favorite dish was the French fries—for the ketchup. They loved ketchup and swathed each fry in as much as it would hold. For lunch the next day the girls bypassed the cold cuts and cheese and ate tomato slices on white bread. We must be willing to be learners, to be flexible, and to be ready for some fun.

Because most American students leave campus and go home, holidays can be particularly lonely for international students. They may even need to find somewhere else to stay. It is a wonderful opportunity to include them in the warmth of your family and to explain the meanings of the holidays and your family's traditions. A Japanese guest at an Easter brunch was full of curiosity. "Why do you have baskets and eggs on the table? Why do you use bunnies?"

▼ America Through Other Eyes ▼

Students come to America assuming that it is a Christian country, and they may become confused reconciling Christianity with American culture. They will be curious about Christianity and may want to ask questions about it. But they will not want it forced upon them.

American life is interesting viewed through different eyes. An American couple visited New Zealand and became friends with a family of New Zealanders. When the New Zealanders subsequently visited the U.S., the two families prepared to go camping. At the supermarket they split up, each person searching for a particular item. Some time later they found one New Zealander standing in front of the baked bean section shaking his head, bewildered. "Americans have too many choices. How many kinds of baked beans do you need?" The supermarket experience disturbed him so much he didn't want to go back.

If you ask an international student a question, he or she will probably be quite honest. Sometimes we will be embarrassed by our own culture.

A Japanese couple in the States on business stood at the window in an American home surveying the backyard: "You live in a park!" they exclaimed.

Internationals help us appreciate some things we take for granted and question the wisdom of other things.

An international friend can literally open the world for our children. Lessons learned in geography, sociology, world trade, and religion aren't forgotten when they come from a person who lives in the country he's talking about. It's one thing to view slides of the Ivory Coast, and quite another to have a guest from that country at your table
.

Many of us have not traveled outside the U.S.; but our children's world is rapidly shrinking. They are likely to journey farther than we have, particularly if they've become fascinated by other cultures they've met in their own homes.

Here's a story that came from a woman matched by International Students, Inc., with an international friend:

"As a single parent with three young children, Jan . . . wasn't sure if she had the time or resources to befriend an international student; but she had the desire to do so. Having recently spent several months overseas, Jan was keenly aware of the hardships of being in a foreign land.

"So . . . [she] signed up to become a Friendship Partner.

"To her surprise and joy, Jan was matched with Sujatha, a graduate student from India who had been raised by a single mother. Sujatha cherished her friendship with Jan and her family and referred to Jan as her 'American mom.' And Jan relished the encouragement Sujatha provided to her as a single parent in raising her children.

" 'I knew it was something God wanted us to do, that we had to look beyond the hurting time we were in,' says Jan. 'I feel like, as a single parent, there's so

much I can't do and so much I wish I could do. But I did what I could, and through that little bit of involvement, God really blessed Sujatha and my family both.' "[9] Single-parent families can both give and receive much from a friend from another culture.

In 1980, the Wilson family's short-term mission trip to Zaire included travel through England, Kenya, and Holland. The children learned to listen to languages and tone differences, memorizing phrases and discussing how words are shaped differently in the mouth. On a flight from Amsterdam to London, a Japanese tourist, eager to practice his limited English, tried to start a conversation with three-year-old Kevin. Kevin finally asked, "What language do you speak? I speak English." Unable to understand or explain, the gentleman slipped a newly made, tiny origami swan through the seats to his new friend. Suddenly no language was necessary.

Our culture values good looks, education, intelligence, and wealth—difficult standards to meet. What do other cultures value? In some countries it is a compliment to say you have gained weight, which implies that one has enough money to buy extra food.

Children profit from seeing that God made us all the same way, with the same basic needs. Not everyone speaks English; people from other countries aren't less intelligent than Americans; and other people love their own countries just as we do ours.

Sometimes Americans are so afraid of offending others that they never interact with people from other cultures. We have found, though, that people from other cultures are aware of nonverbal messages, and a loving, caring heart will be properly perceived and received by nearly anyone.[10] And a smile is a smile the world over. With our children, we will be the learners. The next wave of world leaders is here in the United States right now. Influence the world and enrich your family table: Go out and meet an international friend.

Tea at Ten
Fortune cookies
Decaffeinated herbal tea

Table Talk:
Read your
fortunes aloud.
Make up a
fortune for each family
member and for yourself.

Breakfast
Margaret's Breakfast
Burritos (remember to
bake the potatoes
the day before)
Fresh fruit
Hot chocolate

Margaret's Breakfast Burritos

Use one of the following:
> *1 12-ounce roll light turkey and*
> *pork sausage*
> *1 pound chorizo sausage*
> *½ pound bacon*
> *1 pound ground beef*

1 4-ounce can Ortega diced jalapeños

Use one of the following:
> *3 white potatoes, baked, peeled, and grated or diced*
> *1 dozen eggs, scrambled with ¼ cup chopped onion*

2 tablespoons margarine
Salt and pepper to taste
1 dozen flour tortillas
Optional: *Green chili salsa*

Fry the meat in a medium skillet and drain. Add ⅓ can jalapeños, or to taste. In another skillet, fry the potatoes or eggs and chopped onion in the margarine. Add salt and pepper to taste.

Meanwhile, warm the tortillas, 6 per stack, wrapped in aluminum foil in the oven for 15 minutes. Work with one stack at a time, leaving the second stack in the oven. Spread the meat and eggs or potatoes in a line ⅓ of the way in on a warm tortilla. Roll into a neat cylinder. Top with green chile salsa if desired. Makes 1 dozen burritos.

If you freeze these, individually wrapped in foil, deep fat fry them to re-heat them. Serves 12-15.

Grilled Chili Pepper Cheeseburgers

⅓ cup finely chopped green onion
3 tablespoons nonfat plain yogurt
1 to 4 tablespoons finely chopped jalapeño peppers
½ teaspoon black pepper
½ teaspoon salt
1 pound lean ground beef
1 pound lean ground turkey
6 ounces Monterey Jack cheese with jalapeño peppers
  (hot pepper cheese), cut into 6 slices
8 Kaiser rolls, split and toasted
Leaf lettuce
Sliced tomato

In a medium bowl combine green onions, yogurt, jalapeño peppers, black pepper, and salt. Add beef and turkey; mix well. Shape mixture into 8 patties about ¾ inch thick. If you don't need all 8 patties, freeze some in a freezer bag with waxed paper placed between each patty. Grill the burgers until no pink remains in center. Turn once. Top each patty with cheese the last 2 minutes of grilling time. Serve on buns with lettuce and tomato. Serves 8.

Table Talk:

If anyone in the family knows another language or is learning one, let him or her be the teacher. Learn to say *hello, good-bye, thank you, please,* and *excuse me* in another language.

All-American Dinner to share with international friends

Grilled Chili Pepper Cheeseburgers (or regular cheeseburgers)
Baked Beans
Potato chips
Watermelon
Apple pie
(Be sure to include red-and-white checked tablecloths and an American flag; add a baseball game before or after the meal.)

Table Talk:
What do you miss most about your country? What adjustments are difficult here? What have you enjoyed the most in America? What are your favorite foods and mealtime customs? (See more Table Talk for internationals in appendix.)

Family Dinner
Swedish Meatballs with Noodles
Mixed vegetables
▼ Sautéed Apples with ice cream

Table Talk:
Learn something about and discuss a religion other than Christianity. On a map or globe find the countries where this religion predominates.

Baked Beans

3 1-pound cans Van Camp beans, undrained
2 onions, sliced
1 cup brown sugar
1 tablespoon dry mustard
½ cup molasses
½ cup chili sauce

Empty one can of beans into a bean pot or 2-quart casserole. Combine all the seasonings and layer ½ of the seasoning mixture onto the beans. Then layer one sliced onion. Repeat layers, ending with beans. Bake at 350° for 1 ½ hours. Serves 8-10.

Swedish Meatballs
(Microwave)

1 pound ground beef
½ cup bread crumbs
2 teaspoons parsley flakes
2 teaspoons minced onion
¼ teaspoon nutmeg
⅛ teaspoon salt (optional)
⅛ teaspoon pepper
⅛ teaspoon cinnamon
1 egg

Combine all meatball ingredients. Mix well. Shape into 18 balls, about ½-inch diameter. Arrange in 9-inch square baking dish. Cover with waxed paper. Microwave for 7 to 8 minutes, or until no longer pink in the center of meatballs. Turn the dish twice during the microwaving time. Drain. Set aside.

Sauce:
2 tablespoons margarine
1 tablespoon cornstarch
1 tablespoon parsley flakes
⅛ teaspoon nutmeg
⅛ teaspoon salt (optional)
½ cup milk
½ cup prepared chicken broth or bouillon
1 8-ounce package wide egg noodles

Place margarine in 4-cup measuring cup. Microwave on medium (70 percent) for 30 seconds. Stir in cornstarch, parsley, nutmeg, and salt. Blend in milk and broth. Microwave on High for 2½-4 minutes, stirring after each minute. Serve meatballs over noodles or rice and top with sauce. Serves 4.

Family Dinner
▼ Chicken and Corn
Tostada Salad
Brownies

Table Talk:
Read excerpts from a letter recently written to the family. Pray for the person/family who wrote it.

▾ CHAPTER 9 ▾

SMALL FRIES

Kids migrate to the kitchen,
for tasty concoctions and
for conversation.

What child doesn't love the kitchen? It is the source of the meals and goodies that keep their bodies healthy and vigorous for growth and mischief. The kitchen is often the most comfortable place for a child to share what's on her heart. Linda Burton says it well:

In my experience, our most important discussions happen in the kitchen. Not in the living room. In the living room, most of us tend to be convivial together. We chat, we banter, we discuss the latest books, and we answer questions about what we have been doing with ourselves lately. But in the kitchen, we pour our guts out.

The kitchen lends itself well to the discussion of important matters. First of all, it offers a captive audience in the form of the cook, who is sort of omnipresently simmering something or stirring something 'until it thickens' (which can be forever).

Secondly, the kitchen smells good, and it is usually by virtue of all four burners going, a warm place to be. For most of us, it is particularly pleasant to discuss important matters amid nice smells and warm air.

Finally, it is often much easier to share our most intimate feelings and heartaches if it *seems* like we are not actually doing it. If what we are doing is dicing the onions or peeling the potatoes—if we are somewhat diverted from the strength of our feelings for a moment—it seems somehow easier to express them. After all, if we become too embarrassed or overwrought, we can simply return to making the salad with vengeance. So the kitchen is often an especially 'safe' place to talk. No one is calling us on the carpet, as it were, to Open-Up-Your-Heart-And-Be-Quick-About-It.

Certainly, the creation of this low-key, cozy atmosphere is therapeutic for adults. But for children, I think it is crucial.[1]

As I was baking chocolate chip cookies after school one afternoon, a new boy on the block came to our door wanting to play with our youngest son. He was a handsome boy of nine or 10, with black hair, brown eyes, and long, thick, black eyelashes. Before engaging Drew, he followed me, led by his nose, into the kitchen.

"My grandmother lets me bake cookies with her," he said cheerfully.

In the next few minutes, as he watched me plop spoonfuls of dough onto the baking sheet, he told me that he hadn't gone to preschool because his real mother had kidnapped him and hid him in the house. He couldn't go anywhere. But his dad found him, and now he lived with his dad and third mom and he had one brother and several stepbrothers and stepsisters. But he obviously had a special grandma; he felt safe with her, and she let him help her bake cookies.

We go to great effort to save time in the kitchen, but there's a sort of time in the kitchen that cannot be sacrificed or replaced. It's a strategic baking cookies or stirring the pot and listening time.

A 15-year-old boy gave his mom a high tribute: "Each morning she sits with me while I eat breakfast. We talk about anything and everything. She isn't refined or elegant or educated. She's a terrible housekeeper. She uses double negatives. But she's interested in everything I do and she always listens to me—even if she's busy or tired!"[2]

The kitchen is a sounding board which we, as parents, should use for all it's worth. Ideal opportunities are those times when we're alone with one child. When those mealtimes arise—whether they are the norm in a single or parent/single-child family, or a rare exception in a large family—small touches, like candlelight or an attractive table setting, convey to the child that you respect her and cherish her company.

Jane is raising a 10-year-old son who taxes the limits of her patience and forgiveness. But she has found that it helps when she goes to bed and awakens praying for him. She is then ready to begin each day with a clean slate toward him. She takes two mugs into his bedroom first thing in the morning—one of coffee and one of hot chocolate. She climbs onto the top bunk while he is waking, and they spend 10 minutes just talking together.

▼ Teaching Table Manners ▼

Table manners don't spring from the air when a child needs them at a dinner in another home, a banquet, a fine restaurant—or on a date. I will never forget facing my first lobster dinner on a date with a young man from Florida. He looked across the table to see me shredding my lobster, cutting it against the grain. "May I help you with that before you make me sick?" he asked.

There is one key point of etiquette that overshadows all others and makes the lack of other manners forgivable: That key point is for a child to be grateful for the meal placed before him. What is the worst that can happen if your family is

invited for a meal in another home? The worst is not spilled milk. The worst is not using the wrong fork or not putting the napkin in one's lap. The worst is surveying the food on one's plate and saying "E-e-e-w-w-w, what's this?" or "I don't like broccoli" or "Do I have to eat this, Mommy?" or "Yuck!!!"

Children don't have to eat everything on their plates, but they shouldn't verbally complain about the food, either at home or away. If they aren't allowed to do it at home, they won't forget and do it somewhere else. Call your children's attention to the work involved in preparing a meal. "Did you see that Mrs. Cook went to the trouble to make homemade bread for us?" "It looks like she picked these flowers from her garden just before we came." "Mr. Cook grilled the meat perfectly." "Isn't it a pleasure to have warm stew on a cold night?"

Parents set the tone for grateful living. Children can learn a more sophisticated complaining from their parents. The family may have enjoyed their evening at Pizza Hut, except for the half of the table conversation wasted on Mom and Dad's debate as to whether the crust was too tough.

On a short-term mission trip when Cal and Mimi's children were small, they were guests of honor in an African mud hut near the Ituri Forest of Zaire. In the center of the home three tables of different heights and widths were pushed together, the irregularities covered by one long white tablecloth.

The five hosts at the head of the table were elders of the church of Nyakunde, godly men held in high esteem.

Behind each of the five seated Wilsons stood an elder's wife, clothed in exuberant print fabric, ready to meet his or her every need.

A faint wave of nausea overcame Mimi as she surveyed the meal: boiled peanuts, elephant ear greens (like spinach), and a boiled mystery meat.

She caught Calvin's eye. Cal was a good sport and had a galvanized stomach. She wasn't worried about Cal. But what about . . . Mimi glanced at the children: Kevin was three, Kyndra was six, and Kurt was nine.

All eyes were on the children. *Was the food acceptable and pleasing?* wondered the elders and their wives. The adult guests would be polite and say it was. But from the children's reactions they would know.

An elder's wife deftly snatched a silver-dollar-sized beetle from Kyndra's fine blond hair and flung it out the window, muttering in Swahili, "How dare you disturb our guest!"

Kyndra glanced sheepishly at Mimi, then began eating her greens. The boys talked quietly as they ate. All was well. She had a new appreciation for the behavior they had encouraged at home around the table. A few words with the children on the path to the banquet ("Just eat what they give you and don't complain") wouldn't have been enough.

Teaching table manners shouldn't be a heavy matter. Introduce one thing at a time over the weeks and months: Pass the dishes counterclockwise, ask the host/hostess if you may be excused, learn to set a table correctly, learn to introduce people to one another. Books like *The Family Book of Manners* by Hermine Hartley can be used as a tool.[3] Make it a game. Have the children guess what the appropriate behavior would be.

Try to keep mealtime a positive time, not a battle of wills, even with a two-year-old who is a picky eater. Establish a few rules, be consistent, and let it flow. Don't be too concerned about children who don't finish their dinner, but don't let them snack before meals. If they are not hungry enough for dinner, they aren't hungry enough for dessert.

Mom should not be a short-order cook. Children can learn to be picky eaters by having their preferences catered to too often. Tired of calling people to the table five times? Try a dinner bell or whistle; better yet, delegate the job to someone else.

▼ The Child as Host or Hostess ▼

Children learn to be hospitable by inviting their friends over (asking Mom first, of course, out of earshot of the prospective guest). It's a great way to get to know your children's friends and perhaps encourage another child who needs some attention.

Family rules also apply to any children who come as visitors. Children learn to respect your rules if they are administered positively and consistently, even if they don't have the same rules, or if they have very few rules, at home. Watch that the host child doesn't take the opportunity to act up at the table or become too silly. If your child is invited to eat at a friend's, trust your child's instincts if he or she seems reluctant to spend time in that home.

The same kindnesses apply to guest children as well as the same rules. When Mimi pours a glass of water for a child, she'll hold her finger under the tap and let it run, saying, "I'm going to get this just as cold as I can for you." In the story from the gospels, Jesus instructs the disciples with a child in His arms, "For whoever gives you a cup of water to drink because of your name as followers of

Christ, truly I say to you, he shall not lose his reward."[4] In the days when Jesus spoke, a cup of cold water meant it had been freshly drawn from the well.

Use a meal to help children empathize with a child with an injury or disability. In one family a child had to wear an eye patch. They held a "patch picnic" where each child had to eat wearing a patch over one eye. If one child has a broken arm, tie up the right arms of each of her guests.

Sometimes a child may host a special adult. To celebrate her first communion, Katy invited her pastor for dinner. She chose to serve fajitas. She and her mom shopped together; then Katy chopped the vegetables while her mom grilled the meat. Katie planned the table setting and served strawberries and ice cream for dessert, with seltzer water to drink. "Katie's going to be a great cook someday," said her mom. Katy is being helped along the way through such opportunities.

▼ Kids in the Kitchen ▼

Cooking is a life skill that some children will thoroughly enjoy and all children will profit from. Encourage children to first learn to cook simple dishes they particularly enjoy instead of taking on an entire meal. Maybe they would like to specialize in cinnamon twists made out of convenience biscuits or in French-bread pizzas. If thoughts of the mess keep you from letting your junior chefs experiment, establish the rule that the mess must be cleaned up (be sure they know how you define "cleaned up") before the dish is eaten.

In a large blended family, one son and one daughter, stepsiblings, took an interest in becoming the family bakers. Helping each other, they've become quite adept, they've had fun, they've treated their family to tasty cookies and cakes, and they've bonded with one another.

▼ Giving a Special Touch ▼

When we show children simple acts of kindness that say "You're special to me," they learn to do the same. Cut orange or apple slices and serve them in a small bowl by the bed as a wake-up treat. Cover a tray or cookie sheet with a pretty cloth napkin or clean dish towel. Serve breakfast in bed to a child who went to bed late.

"When a child senses he belongs to the family, he has a security that nothing else can give. He has the ability to stand against the cries of the crowd, entering the world strong and with the ability to love and accept others."[5]

In the warmth of the kitchen with a listening cook, at the table with family and friends, and through his cooking contributions to the family, a child senses the belonging he needs so much.

Tea at Ten
Animal crackers
Decaffeinated herbal
tea

Table Talk:
Prepare a tea for
two children by
themselves. This
can be especially
beneficial after a
conflict between the two
children has been
resolved. The tea time
says they fought, but
they're still friends.
"Behold, how good and
how pleasant it is for
brothers to dwell
together in unity!"[6]

Breakfast
Breakfast Pizza
Fruit juice

Breakfast Pizza

1 12-ounce roll light turkey/pork sausage
1 roll refrigerated pizza crust dough
1 cup frozen, shredded hash brown potatoes, thawed
1 cup (4 ounces) shredded, sharp cheddar, Swiss, or Monterey
 Jack cheese
5 eggs (or egg substitute)
¼ cup milk
⅛ teaspoon pepper
2 tablespoons Parmesan cheese, grated

Preheat oven to 425°. Cook sausage in a skillet until browned.
Drain off excess fat. Spread dough in a 12-inch pizza pan treated
with nonstick spray. Spoon sausage over crust. Distribute
potatoes evenly over the sausage. Top with cheese. In a bowl
whisk together eggs, milk, and pepper. Pour into crust. Sprinkle
Parmesan cheese over all. Bake for 20 minutes. Serves 6-8.
    Great for a children's sleep over.

Spaghetti Zatoni Casserole

1 10 ¾-ounce can tomato soup
1 8-ounce can tomato sauce
1 4-ounce can sliced mushrooms, drained
1 8-ounce can whole kernel corn, including juice
¼ cup pitted ripe olives, drained and chopped
1 pound ground beef, browned
½ pound spaghetti, broken in half and cooked
*   until just tender, rinsed, and drained*
1 cup (4 ounces) grated cheddar cheese
1 green pepper, chopped
1 medium onion, chopped
1 clove garlic, minced
3 tablespoons vegetable oil

Combine first 8 ingredients, only using ½ cup of the cheddar cheese. Chop the green peppers, onions, and garlic and sauté in vegetable oil about 5 minutes and add to the other ingredients. Pour into a 3-quart casserole dish, treated with nonstick spray. Sprinkle the remaining cheddar cheese on top. Bake uncovered at 350° for 40-45 minutes. Serves 8.

Table Talk:
Parents, how do you help people by the work you do? Children, how can you help other students and teachers at school?

Family Dinner
Red Dinner Night
(Use red napkins and red paper plates and cups)
Spaghetti Zatoni Casserole

Cooked beets or carrot sticks and radishes
Raspberry gelatin salad
▼ Cherry Delight

Table Talk:
Who has been your favorite teacher and why?

131

Family Dinner

▼ Chicken Chili
Bread sticks
Flower Pot Sundae

Table Talk:

Read part of a newspaper article and discuss the issue involved.

Family Dinner

Pizza Fish Fillets
Fettuccine
Tossed salad
Sherbet

Table Talk:

Tell about the main character in a book you're reading and the challenge he or she is facing.

Flower Pot Sundae

Buy some tiny clay flower pots. Run them through the dish washer. Put a muffin paper in the bottom of each. Fill each pot with vanilla ice cream. Sprinkle crushed Oreo cookies (tops and bottoms, not filling) on top. Stick a plastic spoon into the ice cream with a plastic red geranium (or other flower) attached to it. Fun for a barbecue with children.

Pizza Fish Fillets

1 ½ pounds fresh or frozen fish fillets (such as haddock, cod, or orange roughy), ½-inch to ¾-inch thick
Nonstick spray coating
½ teaspoon lemon-pepper seasoning
2 cups fresh mushrooms, sliced
1 medium green pepper, chopped (1 cup)
1 medium onion, chopped
¼ cup water
1 8-ounce can pizza sauce
½ cup shredded part-skim mozzarella cheese (2 ounces)
1 12-ounce package spinach (or regular) fettuccine

Thaw fish, if frozen. Cut the fish into 6 serving-sized pieces. Spray a 2-quart rectangular baking dish with nonstick coating. Measure the thickness of the fish. Place fish in the prepared baking dish, tucking under any thin edges. Sprinkle with the lemon-pepper seasoning.

Bake fish, uncovered, in a 450° oven until fish just flakes easily with a fork (allow 6 to 9 minutes per ½ inch thickness). Drain off any liquid.

Meanwhile, in medium saucepan combine mushrooms, green pepper, onion, and pizza sauce and ¼ cup water. Bring to a boil, then simmer 5 minutes.

Spoon sauce over fish. Sprinkle with cheese. Bake 1 minute more or until cheese is melted. Serve on fettuccine. Makes 6 main-dish servings.

Grandma Aziz's Apple Cake

2 cups sugar
1 cup vegetable oil (a "light" oil such as Canola works fine)
4 eggs (or egg substitute)
¼ cup orange juice
2 ½ teaspoons vanilla
3 cups flour
3 teaspoons baking powder
½ teaspoon salt
1 cup chopped nuts
Powdered sugar for topping

Filling:
2 ½ cups tart apples, peeled and diced
1 teaspoon cinnamon

Family Dinner
▼ Black Bean Mexican Pizza
Cottage cheese, mandarin orange sections, and pineapple tidbits
Grandma Aziz's Apple Cake

Table Talk:
Let a child who plays an instrument give a brief concert, one child per night.

133

Kids Cook
Glazed Fruit
Sandwiches (For breakfast,
camping, or dessert)
▼ Orange and Spice
Scented Sugar (For a
teacher's Christmas gift)

Beat first 5 ingredients at medium-high speed for 1 minute. Combine dry ingredients, then blend with first mixture. Fold in nuts. Spread ⅓ batter in a bundt pan sprayed with nonstick spray. Combine filling ingredients, and alternate mixtures ending with batter. Bake for 50 minutes at 350°. Let stand 10 minutes, then remove cake from the pan. Cool and sprinkle with powdered sugar.

Glazed Fruit Sandwiches

1 21-ounce can cherry, blueberry, or apple pie filling
1 16-ounce loaf cinnamon bread
¼ cup butter or margarine, softened

Spread 2-3 tablespoons pie filling on one side of half of the bread slices; top with remaining bread slices. Spread one side of each sandwich with butter. Place each sandwich buttered side down in a cast-iron skillet. Cook over medium heat 1 to 2 minutes or until lightly browned. Butter top side of each sandwich; turn and cook 1 to 2 minutes. Serve with remaining pie filling, if desired. Serves 8.

Sandwiches can be served for dessert or breakfast. Great for camping. Easy for the junior chef.

▾ CHAPTER 10 ▾

PORTABLE MEALS AND EATING OUT

Quality family time is possible anywhere.

It's Mom's birthday, and the family is out to dinner to honor her at a casual Southwestern restaurant. They are splurging on an hors d'oeuvre: a large onion sliced and fried with a dipping sauce. Suddenly Dad rummages in a paper sack he's brought and pulls out dinosaur party hats, which he passes around to Mom and the two kids. Mom, embarrassed but in the spirit of the occasion, is glad that they're in a booth in the back. Dad gives a dinosaur hat to their waitress, requesting that she wear it. Other waiters and waitresses gather around, wanting their dinosaur hats, too. Dad pulls out party toys and passes them around. And all the attention makes Mom feel she's growing younger this evening, not older.

▾ Going Out for Dinner ▾

Statistics show that American families are eating out more often every year. "The share of food dollars spent on food service increased from 25 percent to 46 percent between 1954 and 1992, even though prices for food prepared outside the home rose 37 percent more than prices for food bought in grocery stores."[1] Fast food accounts for the most growth, but casual, come-as-you-are-and-bring-the-kids restaurants are booming nationwide as aging baby boomers eat out with the family in tow.

"Some economists think that as the younger generation ages they will continue to spend more of their food dollars away from home."[2] If that is the case, families must make the most of these away-from-home, team-building times.

If you have young children and are choosing to eat out, select a restaurant with noise and activity: Open kitchens, costumes, and barbecue grills give children something to watch. The main cause of cranky kids is a long wait for the food to be served. Give young children a snack before you leave home, or go prepared with bread sticks or Cheerios and a small cup of juice or milk. You may want to cut the meal down to one or two courses. Save a small bag of quiet toys only for restaurant use. Include crayons or markers so that older children can color a place mat or napkin to give to the waitress as a thank you.

If possible, dine early and beat the rush so food is served faster and waitresses have more time to give attention to the children. Cafeterias—"the place where you push the tray along," as one child calls them—cater to the needs of a family with young children: Children can see what they're selecting, and you avoid the premeal wait.

A single mom and her son often choose a restaurant that attracts seniors. The food is tasty and nutritious, and they both bask in the attention they receive. She is told what a fine mother she is, and he, with a pat on the shoulder, is assured what a fine, growing lad he is.

Dining out is a great time for refining table manners. Let children give their order themselves, even if they are young and you have chosen what they will be eating. Teach them how to make eye contact, how to speak directly to the person taking the order, and how to thank the server when the food is brought to the table.

Young children may like dressing in a costume appropriate to a theme restaurant. When visiting a Mexican restaurant, for example, boys might wear bright shirts and the girls might wear full skirts and paper flowers in their hair. Mimi found that the employees in ethnic restaurants always came by to talk to the children when they could see the children had made special preparations for their evening out.

If the menu includes items with non-English names, try to learn what at least one term means on each restaurant visit. Set an example for the children by trying new foods, discreetly offering them tastes.

While you wait, read from a book of humorous columns or anecdotes or jokes. Or you can play games like "I'm thinking of something in this room that starts with an *r*—what is it?"

Remember that the goal is to enjoy being together. If Mom and Dad need to talk with each other, perhaps they need to go out another night, alone. When the budget can stand it, it's a nice change to have a family dinner out, away from the telephone and kitchen chores, in a new environment. It's fun to share that experience, and it tends to put everyone on their best behavior.

A casual-dining restaurant is usually a notch above fast food in both price and in nutrition. If your meals tend toward fast food, bring the food home sometimes and supplement it with cut-up vegetables, rice, or fruit to improve the food value.

▼ Campfire Cuisine ▼

Nothing outshines camping for family comradeship, teamwork, and fun. My thoughts were along those lines as I fell asleep listening to two of our sons whispering in the dark in their nearby pup tent. The males in our family have camped for years in conjunction with Scouting, but not me. When they finally persuaded me to go, it was on the condition that they set up camp, pack up camp, cook, and clean up. They did, and I realized I was missing out on a lot of the fun!

What would tribal peoples think of us if they knew we go on vacation, at some trouble and expense, for the thrill of cooking potatoes in the coals much like they do? Somehow tasks that seem quite ordinary in the kitchen become an adventure in the coals of a campfire at the edge of the wilderness at night.

Someone generally emerges as chief camp cook, perhaps one who wouldn't touch a pot at home. But it takes a group effort to get the meal on the table. Food can be partially prepared at home. Meat can be frozen in marinade, for example, then transported frozen in a lock-top bag, marinating as it thaws. Grill the meat for fajitas or to eat as is. Kabobs can be prepared the same way.

Ears of corn can be roasted in their husks in coals that have been allowed to burn down and then moved to one side. Moisture in the husk helps steam the corn. One of the beauties of camping is that you get away from appliances and timers of all kinds.

Cook a hobo dinner. In double-thickness, heavy-duty aluminum foil, layer a hamburger patty, sliced onions, and sliced potatoes. Wrap securely and cook the packet in the coals. Canned vegetables can be cooked right in the can, with the lid open but still slightly attached to keep out ashes. Be careful at all times when kids are working or playing around a campfire.

Campfires are for talking and singing and storytelling. Divide the family and sing rounds. Scan your memories for your experiences in the outdoors as a child. Read Psalm 8 aloud and see what constellations you can spy. What is man's position in the scheme of this creation?

Start your own camping traditions. Kurt and Lori Wilson bring with them cheese sandwiches wrapped in heavy foil to cook in the coals while they set up camp.

There are a wide variety of foods that are easy to transport, store, and prepare on a camping trip: individual cereal boxes, coffee cakes, juices, bagels and cream cheese, granola bars, fruit, oatmeal packets, Rice-a-Roni boxed dinners, flavored coffee, and hot chocolate. Use a separate cooler for items you bring frozen that you want to thaw slowly—and don't open it more than necessary. If you freeze water in milk containers to make ice for the cooler, you will have extra water when it thaws.

Are s'mores not rich enough for you? Try spreading peanut butter on the bottom graham cracker, then layer on chocolate chips, roasted marshmallows, and the graham cracker cap.

▾ Condos, Cabins, and Motels ▾

Family dining at a condo or cabin takes forethought to be sure you have the food you want on hand but not too much to pack. Plan your menus with careful thought to refrigeration needs. If you'll have access to an oven, take frozen entrées in a cooler (from your once-a-month plan) and use them as they thaw. The object is to provide inexpensive family meals and minimize cooking time.

In preparation for this book, I visited Mimi in Quito, where we had the joy of planning an escape to a hacienda in the Andes to write. We sat on twig furniture on a lawn bordered by many exotic flowers—Lily of the Nile, Red Hot Pokers, and orchids. We laughed a lot and assured ourselves we were being very productive.

Kevin Wilson and I joined Cal and Mimi each morning in their room for breakfast of homemade bread, typical fresh fruit—granadilla, tree tomatoes, or tangerines—oatmeal packets, and instant flavored coffees made with water boiled in an electric coffee pot.

It poured all Saturday night. We had planned to stay until Monday, but a mud slide that night fouled the village water supply, and Sunday morning found us without water for breakfast. The hacienda staff said the problem would be resolved by midafternoon, but Cal and Mimi had lived there long enough to know better.

As Kevin and I arrived for Sunday's breakfast, a bit soiled behind the ears from lack of a shower, Cal was pouring water into the oatmeal as usual. "Where did you get that water?" I wondered.

He chuckled, "Don't ask." I passed on the coffee and oatmeal.

Breakfasts like these are simple for a condo or even a motel. Other ideas for condo breakfasts and lunches include fixings for ham, tuna, or peanut butter sandwiches and for chicken salad brought in the cooler and then served in pita bread. Bring chef salad ingredients, with as much moisture as possible removed, in lock-top plastic bags, and a bottle of salad dressing. Nachos, spaghetti, and chicken breasts grilled and served with Rice-a-Roni are all good supplements to your frozen entrées. Divide snacks into individual lock-top bags for daily portions: celery and carrot sticks, granola bars, fruit snacks, animal crackers, and fig bars.

Two families vacationed in Florida together and used much of this cuisine in the menus they carefully planned before the trip. The moms assumed the children didn't particularly care about the meals. But when the parents asked their children afterward to write down memories from the trip, they each included from memory the meals they'd eaten each day.

Some of the best family times can be times away, together, free from the distractions of telephone, television, the neighborhood, and everyday demands. The miserable car trips, the air-conditioning problem in the motel room, the family of eight who moved into your favorite camping spot—these memories will fade, or at least become part of the reservoir of shared family humor. The good memories of family times out or away are worth the planning and effort.

Trail Jambalaya

1 cup long-grain rice, uncooked
1 tablespoon dried onion flakes
1 tablespoon dried parsley flakes
2 teaspoons beef-flavored bouillon granules
¼ teaspoon black pepper
¼ teaspoon garlic powder
¼ teaspoon dried thyme
⅛ teaspoon ground red pepper
2 cups water
1 8-ounce can tomato sauce
½ pound smoked sausage, cut into ¼ inch slices

Combine long-grain rice and next 7 ingredients in a heavy-duty, lock-top plastic bag. To serve, combine rice mix, 2 cups water, and tomato sauce in a Dutch oven. Bring to a boil; cover, reduce heat, and simmer 20 minutes. Stir in smoked sausage, and cook until mixture is thoroughly heated. Serves 4.

Tea at Ten
Cinnamon toast
Decaffeinated herbal tea

Table Talk:
Read a poem expressive of
the current season.

Breakfast (Camping)
▼ Camper's Oatmeal
Fruit juice

Table Talk:
When do you feel
most peaceful?

Family Dinner (Camping)
Trail Jambalaya
Canned fruit cocktail

Table Talk:
Share a memory that goes
way, way back in
your childhood.

Taco Soup
For camping *or* staying home

1 pound ground beef (or ground chicken or turkey)
½ cup onion, chopped
2 cups water
2 16-ounce cans Mexican-style stewed tomatoes, cut up
2 8-ounce cans tomato sauce
1 envelope taco seasoning mix
2 16-ounce cans kidney beans
Tortilla chips
Grated cheese
Sour cream
Hot sauce

Brown meat with onions and drain. For use when camping, pre-freeze the meat/onion mixture and take it camping frozen. To serve, add water, stewed tomatoes, tomato sauce, taco seasoning mix, and kidney beans to thawed meat mixture in a large pot. Heat to boiling and simmer 10 minutes.

Crush tortilla chips in the bottom of individual serving bowls. Pour soup over the chips. Top with grated cheese, sour cream and hot sauce. Serves 6-8.

Sweet-and-Sour Pork

1 ½ pounds pork tenderloin, cut into 1-inch cubes
½ cup onion, chopped
1 tablespoon vegetable oil
1 8-ounce can pineapple chunks
¼ cup brown sugar, firmly packed
1 tablespoon corn starch
½ teaspoon salt
⅓ cup white vinegar
1 tablespoon soy sauce
2 tablespoons catsup
½ cup water
1 large green pepper, sliced thin
Chow mein noodles

In a large skillet or saucepan brown pork cubes and onion in vegetable oil. Drain pineapple, reserving juice. In a small mixing bowl combine brown sugar, cornstarch, salt, pineapple juice, vinegar, soy sauce, catsup, and water. Pour over pork mixture, stirring over medium heat until sauce thickens. Cover and simmer 30 minutes. Stir in pineapple chunks and green pepper. Cover and cook 3 minutes. Serve over chow mein noodles. Serves 4.

Family Dinner

Sweet-and-Sour Pork
▼Hawaiian Fruit Salad
Snow Peas

Table Talk:

What do you like or dislike about spending the night away from home? What do you miss about home when you're gone?

▼ RECIPES ▼

Butter Rolls

8 cups flour
1 cup sugar
1 tablespoon salt
4 eggs, beaten
1 package dry yeast
2 cups milk
1 cup (2 sticks) butter

Soften yeast in ½ cup warm water, and add 1 tablespoon of sugar. Mix all dry ingredients in mixing bowl. Melt butter, add milk and beaten eggs. Add liquid to the dry mixture, including the yeast, and mix together until smooth. Refrigerate overnight.

At least 3 hours before serving, remove dough from refrigerator. Shape dough into rolls approximately 2 inches in diameter and let rise 1 to 1 ½ hours. If desired, with sharp scissors cut a cross in the top of each roll. Bake 20-25 minutes at 400° or until done. Makes about 3 dozen.

Camper's Oatmeal

2 cups quick-cooking oatmeal, uncooked
½ cup chopped dates or chopped dried apples*
¼ cup chopped pecans
¼ cup brown sugar, firmly packed
½ teaspoon ground cinnamon
½ cup instant nonfat dry milk powder

Combine all ingredients in a heavy-duty, lock-top plastic bag. To serve, spoon desired amount of oatmeal into bowl and pour boiling water over it, barely covering the oatmeal mixture. Stir and let stand 2 minutes. For thinner oatmeal, add more boiling water; to thicken, add more oatmeal mixture. Yield: 3 cups oatmeal mix.

* 2 9-ounce packages orchard fruit snack mix may be substituted. Also good for a quick family breakfast!

▼ Desserts ▼

Cherry Delight

Crust:
2 cups flour
½ cup brown sugar
1 cup margarine, melted
1 cup pecans, chopped
Filling:
8 ounces light cream cheese
1 cup powdered sugar
1 teaspoon vanilla
1 pint whipping cream or 2 cups Cool Whip
1 30-ounce can cherry pie filling

Preheat oven to 400°. Mix together the crust ingredients and press in bottom of a 9x13-inch pan. Bake 15 minutes. Use a fork to crumble crust into pieces. Cool.

Soften the cream cheese. Mix with powdered sugar and vanilla. Beat the whipping cream until it keeps soft peaks, or use Cool Whip. Fold into cream cheese mixture. Pour over crumb-crust mixture. Spread the cherry pie filling on top. Refrigerate.

Chocolate Chip Cake

2 cups flour
1 cup dark brown sugar, packed
½ cup sugar
3 teaspoons baking powder
1 teaspoon salt
½ teaspoon baking soda
½ cup shortening
1 ¼ cups milk
3 eggs
½ cup semisweet chocolate pieces
1 ½ teaspoons vanilla

Heat oven to 350°. Spray two 9x1 ½-inch round layer pans with nonstick spray. Measure all ingredients except chocolate chips into mixing bowl. Blend ½ minute on low, scraping bowl constantly. Beat 3 minutes on high. Fold in chocolate chips. Divide between the two pans. Bake 40-45 minutes or until a wooden pick inserted in the center comes out clean. Cool. Spread Butterscotch Filling (recipe below) between the two layers. Sprinkle nuts over the filling. Spread Chocolate Chip Glaze (recipe below) over top of the cake.

Butterscotch Filling for Chocolate Chip Cake

½ cup light brown sugar, packed
¼ cup cornstarch
¼ teaspoon salt
½ cup water
1 tablespoon butter
Optional: ½ cup walnuts, chopped

Stir together sugar, cornstarch, and salt in small saucepan. Stir in water. Cook on medium high, stirring constantly, until mixture thickens and boils. Boil and stir one minute. Blend in butter. Cool.

Chocolate Chip Glaze for Chocolate Chip Cake

½ cup semisweet chocolate pieces
2 tablespoons butter
1 tablespoon light corn syrup

Melt over low heat and drizzle over cake.

Chocolate Sauce

1 12-ounce package semisweet chocolate chips
½ pint whipping cream

Melt together over low heat or in the top of a double boiler. Do not boil. Beat to get out the lumps. Refrigerate if desired.

Fresh Fruit Tart

Crust:
1 cup flour
1 tablespoon sugar
⅛ teaspoon salt
5 tablespoons vegetable shortening

3 tablespoons butter, unsalted
3 tablespoons ice water
Filling:
8 ounces cream cheese, softened at room temperature
¼ cup sugar
2 ½ teaspoons fresh lemon juice
½ cup whipping cream, whipped
2 kiwis, peeled and sliced
½ pint fresh strawberries, hulled and halved
¼ pint fresh blueberries
½ 11-ounce can mandarin orange segments, drained
¼ cup apricot preserves
1 tablespoon water

For crust: Combine flour, sugar, and salt in medium bowl. Add shortening and butter and cut in until mixture resembles coarse meal. Mix in enough water by tablespoons to form dough that just comes together. Gather dough into ball; flatten into disk. Wrap in plastic and refrigerate 30 minutes.

     Roll out dough on lightly floured surface to ⅛ inch thick round. Transfer dough into 9-inch diameter tart pan with a removable bottom. Trim and crimp edges. Refrigerate 30 minutes.

     Preheat oven to 375°. Line tart with foil. Fill crust with dried beans, uncooked rice or pie weights. Bake 15 minutes. Remove foil and beans. Bake until golden brown, about 10 minutes longer. Transfer to a cooling rack and cool completely.

For filling: Using an electric mixer, beat cream cheese, sugar, and lemon juice in a large bowl until well blended. Beat the whipping cream until it holds soft peaks. Fold whipped cream into filling. Spread filling into the cooled tart shell. Cover and refrigerate overnight.

     Arrange fruit in concentric circles on top of filling. (This dessert can be prepared up to 3 hours ahead. Refrigerate.) Bring preserves and 1 tablespoon water to a boil in a small, heavy saucepan or microwave. Brush glaze over fruit and serve. Serves 8-12.

Lemon Cake

Cake:
1 package lemon cake mix with pudding in the mix (or one lemon cake mix and l box lemon instant pudding)
4 eggs (or egg substitute)
¾ cup water
¾ cup vegetable oil
Glaze:
¼ cup orange juice
1 ½ cups powdered sugar

Preheat oven to 350°. Combine 4 cake ingredients and beat for 4 minutes at medium speed. Bake in 9x13x2-inch pan treated with nonstick spray for 40 minutes at 350°. While the cake is still hot, prick it all over with a toothpick. In a bowl, blend the orange juice and sugar until smooth. Pour glaze over cake.

Orange and Spice Scented Sugar

1 cup sugar
1 tablespoon orange peel, grated
½ teaspoon cinnamon
¼ teaspoon nutmeg
¼ teaspoon cardamom
⅛ teaspoon ginger

Heat oven to 200°. Thoroughly mix all ingredients in 8x8x2-inch baking pan. Bake, stirring occasionally, 15 minutes. Cool pan on wire rack.

Store in tightly covered jar in cool, dry place. Use to sweeten coffee, tea, applesauce, fresh apples, or sprinkle on pancakes, waffles, or French toast. Makes about one cup.

This is a nice gift item. For example: As a Christmas gift for teachers, use small jar (such as maraschino cherry jars) with a decorative ribbon and label.

Pistachio Dessert

Crust:
1 cup flour
½ cup margarine, melted
1 cup pecans
Filling:
8-ounce package cream cheese
1 cup powdered sugar
1 cup Cool Whip
2 packages pistachio instant pudding
3 cups milk
Mix the crust ingredients and press into an 8x11-inch pan. Bake 20 minutes at 350°. Cool.

Mix the cream cheese and powdered sugar together at low speed. Fold in Cool Whip. Spread this mixture over the crust. Mix the pudding and milk thoroughly and spread on the above. Refrigerate. You can use instant chocolate pudding instead of pistachio. Serves 8-10.

Pumpkin Chip Cookies

1 cup butter or margarine
1 cup brown sugar, packed
1 cup sugar
1 egg
1 teaspoon vanilla
2 cups flour
1 cup old-fashioned Quaker oats
1 teaspoon baking soda
1 teaspoon cinnamon
½ teaspoon salt
*1 cup solid pack pumpkin (not pumpkin pie filling)
*1 cup semisweet chocolate chips or raisins

Preheat oven to 350°. Cream butter and sugars and add the egg and vanilla and mix thoroughly. Combine dry ingredients. Alternate adding dry ingredients and pumpkin to the creamed mixture. Stir in chocolate chips or raisins. Drop by spoonfuls onto a lightly greased baking sheet. Bake 20-25 minutes. Remove and cool on racks. Makes about 3 dozen cookies.

Soft and chewy—send to your favorite college student.
* One 12-ounce package of chocolate chips and one 16-ounce can of pumpkin make two batches.

Sautéed Apples

4 small apples (such as Golden Delicious)
2 tablespoons butter or margarine
2 teaspoons cinnamon
2 tablespoons brown sugar
Optional: *vanilla ice cream*

Peel (if desired), core, and thinly slice apples (12-16 slices per apple). Melt butter with cinnamon and brown sugar in a medium skillet over medium heat. Sauté apples for 1 minutes on each side or until tender but not mushy. Serve plain or over vanilla ice cream. Serves 4-6.

▼ Entrees ▼

Black Bean Mexican Pizza

Crust:
1 10-ounce can refrigerated pizza crust (Food Club or Pillsbury)
Topping:
1 15-ounce can black beans, drained and rinsed
3 tablespoons olive or vegetable oil
2 tablespoons chopped fresh cilantro or parsley
1 teaspoon cumin
Pinch of ginger
½ teaspoon salt
1 teaspoon hot red pepper sauce
½ teaspoon minced garlic
2 cups grated Monterey Jack and Colby cheese
1 2 ¼-ounce can sliced ripe olives, drained
½ cup diced green pepper
1 cup thick and chunky salsa

Heat oven to 425°. Treat 12-inch pizza pan or 9x13-inch pan with nonstick spray. Unroll dough and place in greased pan; starting at center, press out with hands. Bake at 425° for 7-10 minutes or until light golden brown.

In food processor bowl with metal blade or in blender, combine beans, oil, cilantro, cumin, ginger, salt, hot red pepper sauce, and garlic; process until smooth, frequently scraping down sides of bowl. Bean mixture can be mashed with fork or potato masher, but it will not be as smooth.

Spread bean mixture over partially baked crust. Sprinkle with cheese, olives, and green pepper. Bake at 425° for 12 minutes or until crust is deep golden brown and cheese is melted.

Serve pizza with salsa. The topping, minus the crust, could be used as a dip with corn chips or crackers. Serves 6-8.

Chicken Chili

1 cup red onion, chopped
2 large celery stalks, chopped
2 tablespoons margarine
1 14 ½-ounce can Mexican-style stewed tomatoes
2 cups water
2 chicken bouillon cubes
1 8-ounce can tomato sauce
1 package chili seasoning
1 16-ounce can kidney beans, drained
1 12-ounce can whole kernel corn, drained
3 cups cooked, diced chicken
Corn chips

In a large pot or saucepan sauté the chopped onion and chopped celery in margarine until transparent. Add the other ingredients in the order given. Bring to a boil, reduce heat and simmer for 30 minutes. Serve with corn chips.

Chicken with a Zip
(A dinner to freeze ahead)

In bag 1:

       6 boneless, skinless chicken breast halves, cut in one-inch strips
       1 cup lemon juice

In bag 2:

       1 cup flour
       1 ½ teaspoons salt
       2 teaspoons paprika
       1 teaspoon pepper

In bag 3:

       2 tablespoons lemon peel, grated
       ½ cup brown sugar
       1 chicken bouillon cube dissolved in ½ cup water

Put all 3 small bags in 1 large bag; label and freeze. When ready to cook, thaw bags. Take chicken out and pat dry. Put it in bag 2 with seasonings and shake. Place one layer deep in a baking dish. Pour contents of bag 3 on top. Bake uncovered 50 minutes at 325°.

    Garnish with lemon and parsley. Also good on a hard roll as a sandwich. May be served at room temperature, hot, or cold.

Chili Mac

1 pound lean ground beef
½ cup onion, chopped
½ cup green pepper, chopped
3 cloves garlic, minced
½ cup water
1 tablespoon chili powder

1 teaspoon ground cumin
1 teaspoon salt
¼ teaspoon pepper
1 16-ounce can Southwestern Chili Tomatoes Diced with Chili Spices
1 15-ounce can kidney beans, drained
1 11-ounce can whole kernel corn, drained
1 8-ounce can tomato sauce
1 6-ounce can tomato paste
2 cups cooked elbow macaroni
1 cup (4 ounces) shredded sharp cheddar cheese

Cook first 4 ingredients in a large Dutch oven over medium-high heat until browned, stirring to crumble beef. Drain well; wipe drippings from pan with paper towels. Return beef mixture to pan; add next 10 ingredients, stirring well. Bring to a boil; cover, reduce heat, and simmer 20 minutes, stirring occasionally. Just before serving, stir in macaroni and heat through. Spoon onto individual serving plates; top with cheese. Serves 8.

Easy Oven Lasagna

¼ pound ground beef or turkey
¾ cup water
4 cups marinara sauce (see recipe below)
8 ounces lasagna noodles, uncooked
1 cup lowfat cottage cheese
¾ cup part-skim mozzarella cheese, sliced
¼ cup grated Parmesan cheese

Preheat oven to 375°. Brown meat in skillet treated with nonstick spray and drain well. Add water and marinara sauce and bring to a boil. Remove from heat. In a 9x13-inch dish layer 1/3 of the sauce, half the uncooked lasagna noodles, half the cottage cheese, half the mozzarella cheese; repeat layers, ending with sauce and Parmesan cheese. The sauce will be runny. Cover with foil and bake 1 hour. Let stand 5-10 minutes before cutting into squares. Makes 6-8 generous servings.

Marinara Sauce

1 clove garlic, minced
1 tablespoon olive oil
2 16-ounce cans unsalted, chopped tomatoes
2 8-ounce cans tomato sauce
1 tablespoon oregano leaves
1 tablespoon chopped parsley

Sauté garlic in olive oil. Add tomatoes and tomato sauce slowly. Stir in oregano and parsley. Bring to a boil and simmer slowly for 20 minutes to 2 hours (the longer the better). Break up the tomatoes with a potato masher or blender and stir occasionally.

This sauce has great versatility. Use it as a pizza sauce and in any other dishes calling for tomato sauce. For a Mexican sauce add ½-1 teaspoon ground cumin and a dash of hot sauce. Makes about 4 cups.

Janie's Chicken Breasts

2 ½ pounds chicken breasts or 6 boneless, skinless chicken breast halves
¼ cup melted margarine
1 cup soda cracker crumbs
1 cup grated Parmesan cheese
Dried parsley flakes

Melt the margarine in a pie plate in the oven as it preheats to 325°. In another pie plate, stir together the cracker crumbs, Parmesan cheese and parsley for color. Roll chicken breasts in melted margarine, then in the crumb mixture. Bake 1 ¼ hours, uncovered in a 9x13-inch pan, at 325° or 40 minutes at 325° for boneless breasts. Serves 6.

London Broil

1 flank steak, about 2 pounds
2 tablespoons salad oil
1 tablespoon parsley flakes
2 cloves garlic, crushed
2 teaspoons salt
2 teaspoons fresh lemon juice
¼ teaspoon black pepper

With a sharp knife trim excess fat from the steak. Wipe with paper towel to dry. Lay the steak on a cutting board and score about ¼ inch down into the meat at an angle across the grain of the meat, at 1-inch intervals. Repeat the scoring at a 90-degree angle, creating small squares between the scores. (Score on one side only.)

Combine salad oil, parsley, garlic, salt, lemon juice, and pepper. Brush mixture over the steak on both sides; let the meat stand (marinate) at least 45 minutes (may be refrigerated for longer marination).

Broil or grill the meat about 4 inches from the heat for 5 minutes. Turn the steak and brush with remaining oil mixture and cook an additional 4 to 5 minutes. The meat will be rare—the only way London Broil should be served.

Remove steak to a cutting board or platter and slice very thinly against the meat grain. You may cut the meat on a diagonal (45 degrees to the cutting board) for larger slices.

Note: In many areas, self-service meat departments sell a cut of beef labeled London Broil which is round steak. To prepare this substitute, after drying meat with paper towel, sprinkle with instant meat tenderizer per the label's instructions. Then proceed as above but leave out the salt. The flank steak cut is preferred over the round steak and will be more flavorful. Serves 4-6.

South of the Border Casserole

2 pounds ground beef
2 10 ½-ounce cans tomato soup
2 10 ½-ounce cans chili beef soup
8 ounces cheddar cheese, grated
1 tablespoon onion, minced
1 12-ounce package corn chips

Brown ground beef and drain. Stir in undiluted soups and onion. Heat thoroughly. Place 2 cups corn chips in bottom of 2 ½ quart casserole dish. Top with half of the meat mixture and half the cheese. Repeat layers and bake at 350° for 25-30 minutes.

Pasta Mornay

1 ¼ cup uncooked pasta, your favorite kind
½ cup zucchini, sliced ⅛-inch thick
⅓ cup frozen peas
2 tablespoons sliced green onion
1 tablespoon margarine
1 tablespoon parsley flakes

¼ teaspoon dried basil
Dash pepper
2 teaspoons flour
½ cup evaporated skim milk
¼ cup Swiss cheese, shredded
4 ounces low-fat ham (or turkey ham), cut into strips

Prepare pasta as directed on package. Drain. In a 1 ½ quart casserole combine zucchini, peas, onion, margarine, parsley, basil, and pepper. Cover. Microwave on high 2-3 minutes or until vegetables are tender, yet crisp, stirring once. Stir in flour; blend in milk. Microwave uncovered on high power 2 ½ to 3 ½ minutes until it bubbles. Stir once, then stir in Swiss cheese, ham, and pasta.. Good warm or chilled. Serves 4.

Country Fried Potatoes

Make from leftover baked potatoes
3 baked white potatoes
½ cup onion, chopped
½ cup green pepper, chopped
½ cup cheddar cheese, grated
Salt and pepper to taste
3 tablespoons butter or margarine
Optional: *Chopped ham, cooked corn, 4 eggs*

Dice the cooked potatoes. In a large skillet over medium heat, sauté the potatoes, onion, and green pepper in butter until the potatoes are a golden brown. Combine cheese with corn and/or eggs. Add to potatoes and cook till heated thoroughly or until eggs are firm and cheese is melted. Stir continually to prevent burning. Serves 4-6.

▾ Salads and Hors D'oeuvres ▾

Chicken and Corn Tostada Salad

Salad:
1 tablespoon olive or vegetable oil
*2 whole chicken breasts, skinned, boned, cut into 2x½-inch strips
½ tablespoon garlic salt
1 16-ounce package frozen corn
1 tomato, chopped
1 15-ounce can black beans, drained and rinsed
5 green onions, thinly sliced including tops
1 medium avocado, peeled and chopped
1 head of lettuce—buttonhead, Boston, or Bibb lettuce
1 small red or green pepper, chopped
2 cups shredded Monterey Jack cheese
3 cups slightly crushed blue-corn or regular tortilla chips
Dressing:
¼ cup cider vinegar or red wine vinegar
3 tablespoons honey
1 ½ teaspoon cumin
¼ teaspoon salt
⅛ teaspoon pepper

Heat oil in skillet and cook chicken about 5 minutes. Transfer to bowl and sprinkle with garlic salt. Cover and refrigerate 30 minutes. Tear lettuce into bite-sized pieces. Add remaining salad ingredients and toss together. In a jar, combine dressing ingredients. Shake well. Pour over salad and toss lightly. Serve over tortilla chips as a main dish. Serves 8-10.
* Chicken breast can be grilled if desired.

164

Sweet-and-Sour Tossed Salad

1 head romaine lettuce, torn into bite-sized pieces
1 small cucumber, sliced
1 avocado, peeled, pitted, and sliced
1 11-ounce can mandarin orange sections, drained
2 tablespoons sliced green onion
Dressing:
¼ cup orange juice
½ cup salad oil
2 tablespoons sugar
2 tablespoons red wine vinegar
1 tablespoon lemon juice
¼ teaspoon salt

Combine lettuce, cucumber, avocado, oranges, and onion. Cover and refrigerate until serving time.

In a covered jar, combine the dressing ingredients. Shake well and refrigerate until serving. Pour over salad and toss. Serves 6.

Janet's Tortilla Hors D'oeurves

2 8-ounce packages light cream cheese, softened
1 small can diced, green chilies
1 small can pitted, diced ripe olives
3 green onions
1 small can diced pimentos
1 tablespoon garlic salt
1 package 8-inch diameter flour tortillas
Salsa for dipping

Mix all ingredients except the tortillas and salsa. Spread each tortilla with the mixture and roll it up. A little cream cheese mixture on the very edge will help it stay rolled. Place the filled tortillas seam-side down in a 9 X 13-inch dish in refrigerator. When ready to serve, slice each tortilla into approximately 6 slices and serve with salsa.

These may be wrapped individually in aluminum foil and frozen. Serves 12.

▼ Vegetables ▼

Corn on the Grill

1 roasting ear of corn per person
Butter
Salt and pepper

Remove the husks from the ears of corn. Wrap each ear separately in heavy-duty aluminum foil. Place the ears on a grill rack over hot coals for 15-20 minutes, turning every 5 minutes. Serve with butter, salt, and pepper.

Criss-Cross Potatoes

6 baking potatoes, washed
2 tablespoons butter
Salt
Paprika

Cut the baking potatoes in half lengthwise. Make ⅛ inch deep diagonal slashes ½ inch apart. Repeat diagonal slashes at a 90-degree angle, forming a criss-cross pattern. Melt butter in a small dish and lightly coat the top surface of the potatoes. Place potato halves on a paper towel on a microwave-proof dish and cook in microwave on high for 25 minutes, turning dish twice (or bake in oven at 400° for 40 minutes). Recoat the top surface of the potatoes with melted butter, sprinkle with salt and paprika, and continue to cook in microwave 5 minutes (or in oven 10 minutes). Serves 6.

Impossible Garden Pie

2 cups zucchini, chopped
1 cup tomatoes, chopped
½ onion, chopped
⅓ cup grated Parmesan cheese
Optional: ½ teaspoon dill weed
1 cup milk
½ cup baking mix
2 eggs
1 teaspoon salt
Pepper to taste

Sprinkle vegetables in 10-inch pie plate sprayed with nonstick spray. Beat remaining ingredients in blender on high for 15 seconds or until smooth. Pour into pie plate and bake at 400° for 35-40 minutes. Let cool for 5 minutes. Cut into 6-8 servings.

TABLE TOPICS

- ▾ Devise a family plan for evacuating your home in an emergency.

- ▾ Role-play appropriate procedures for answering the phone and taking messages.

- ▾ Take a saying like "Start at the top and work down." Think of as many applications for it as you can.

- ▾ Tell us about one thing you started today and one thing you finished.

- ▾ What worries you most?

- ▾ Of what are you proudest?

- ▾ Put a family photo album in the center of the table and reminisce.

- ▾ If you could do anything you want, what would it be?

- ▾ Give a sincere compliment to the person on your right.

- ▾ What responsibilities do you think parents have to their children?

- ▾ Which of your friends' parents do you respect most and why?

- ▾ What would you most like to change about yourself?

- ▾ With company: Read off a list of state capitals. Going around the table, have each person try to match the state with the capital.

▼ Start a story. After a few sentences stop and ask the next person to add on to the story and so around the table.

▼ With young children: Tell us about the picture you drew today.

▼ With young children: Sing a simple chorus.

▼ Read an ongoing story. See Jim Trelease's *The New Read-Aloud Handbook*.[1]

▼ Discuss positively what chores are working at home and what are not.

▼ Discuss upcoming events or life-style changes that will affect your lives (i.e., Mom working full time, Grandpa's illness, an upcoming guest).

▼ What is one new thing you'd like to try?

▼ Where is one place you'd like to go?

▼ For parents: How can you help people at work?

▼ Let a child who plays an instrument give a brief concert; one child per night.

▼ Ask for five favorite and five most dreaded phrases. This is the response Dolores Curran got from a group of fourth- and fifth-graders. Favorites: I love you; you can stay up late; yes; you can go; time to eat. Least favorites: How many times do I have to tell you? I don't care who says so; don't argue with me; because I say so; ask Dad.[2]

▼ Mom and Dad tell what they worried about most and what they liked most when they were children.

▼ Ask grandparents to reminisce about legends and colorful characters in their families.

▼ Take five minutes to brainstorm the answer to this question: What are our family traditions?

▼ Play family trivia: Where did Dad and Mom meet? How many second cousins do you have? What was the name of our first pet? and so forth.

▼ Talk about salaries. Give five or six examples of average earnings for various occupations. Do wages necessarily match the value or significance of the work done?

▼ Share a memory that goes way back in your childhood.

▼ What is the best thing that happened to you today? The worst thing?

▼ What is the funniest thing that happened to you today?

▼ How did you see God at work today?

▼ Bring a newspaper clipping and discuss a character quality it exemplified (i.e., greed, courage, disregard for human life).

▾ Read excerpts from a letter recently written to the family.

▾ What was the most interesting thing you learned today?

▾ Tell about the main character in a book you're reading and the challenge he or she is facing.

▾ Discuss a movie or television show that you have all watched.

▾ Who-Does-It-Belong-to Night: Bring out of a bag out-of-place objects one by one. Who does it belong to? (Keep it light.) Does it work? Do you want to keep it? Then you may be excused to quickly put it away.

▾ Why are some people liked and some are not?

▾ What is the difference between natural talents and spiritual gifts?

▾ What would be your ideal vacation?

▾ What is your favorite Christmas decoration? How did it become special to you?

▾ Find and read a poem expressive of the current season.

▾ Tell something someone said today that made you feel good about yourself.

▾ If you were the opposite sex, what would be the hardest adjustment?

- If you could change one physical feature, what would it be?

- What is/was your nickname in school?

- For adults: If you could change your profession, what would you choose now?

- What characteristics do you see in you that came from your father/mother?

- What qualities would you like to emulate from your parents/relatives?

- If you had $1,000, what would you do with the money?

- What was your most frightening experience?

- Discuss faith and good works.

- Discuss God's sovereignty versus man's free will.

- Discuss concepts like the exchange rate or the electoral college.

- Discuss what should be done in the event of a car accident.

▼ With International Friends ▼

▼ Discuss how his or her money corresponds with U.S. currency according to the exchange rate.

▼ What games do children play in your country? Youths? Adults?

▼ What differences have you observed between schools here and there?

▼ In what ways do you hope to apply the education you are receiving here when you return home?

▼ Teach us to say some words in your language.

▼ What is your favorite food in your country? In our country?

▼ How do people in your culture worship? What are some of their religious customs?

▼ What did you know about Christianity before you came here?
Has anything you've learned about the Christian faith while you've been here surprised you? What?

▼ How large is your family? What sort of work do your parents do?

▼ Who are the prominent people in your country?

▼ How do people greet one another and say good-bye in your country?

▼ From Ungame Cards[3] ▼

▼ Tell about a family tradition that you enjoy.

▼ What was your favorite childhood storybook? Why did you like it?

▼ Complete the sentence: "My favorite time of day is . . ."

▼ If you could spend one whole day with your best friend, what would you like to do?

▼ How do you think your mother (father) would describe you?

▼ In what ways does TV influence your life?

▼ Which holiday has the most meaning for you and why?

▼ How does music affect your life?

▼ Share an experience of embarrassment.

▼ Tell about a mistake you made recently.

▼ When do you feel most peaceful?

▼ Complete the sentence "I hope . . . "

▾ GIVING YOUR BEST ▾
A Mealtime Story

As the long rays of the evening sun filtered through the towering trees in the tropical jungle of Zaire, an old car entered an isolated mission station carrying a large family of missionaries. The trunk lid had been removed, and the children who didn't fit inside the car were riding in the back. They were covered with dirt from the dusty road.

Mimi, a child then, stood in the doorway with her mother, watching the family drive into the yard. Her mother whispered, "They're as poor as church mice; let's give them some of our things." Mimi wondered what church mice ate. As she thought about it, she concluded that the situation must be serious, serious enough to go through the toy box and share some of her toys. While the family ate in the dining room, Mimi chose several broken things, including an old doll that was missing a leg, windup toys that had lost their spring, and a puzzle with missing pieces. The children seemed delighted with her castoffs. As the car disappeared down the road that night, the children were playing with their new toys in the trunk of the car.

Mimi turned to her mother, hoping for a compliment. "Didn't they like my things?" Mimi will never forget her mother's answer, in a voice of longing rather than anger.

"Only you know if you have given your best." Her mother turned to enter the house and resume washing the dishes. Mimi was deeply impressed by the remark. She knew that her mom had given her best to Jesus, and that she wanted Mimi to understand the joy that comes with such a gift. Nothing more was said.

Years later, while in a private high school, Mimi met a missionary girl with very few clothes to wear. Her own closet was full, so Mimi decided to give the girl half of her wardrobe. She pulled out every other dress, and was doing fine parting with dresses that did not fit well and dresses that were not the right color, until she came to her white wool dress. It was Mimi's favorite, and she always received compliments wearing it. Her mother's comment played through her mind. Only Mimi would know if she had given her best.

Mimi snatched the dress off the hanger and included it on the growing stack of give-away clothes.

Later that week, Mimi received a package in the mail with no return address. She opened it and found a gorgeous white wool dress. It was as if God was saying, "I noticed that you gave me your best." Mimi knew that she would not always receive something exactly like what she had given. But she also knew that God wanted to teach her a lesson about giving, and that no gift to God goes unnoticed by Him.

Years later, one hot summer day, in a suburb of Denver, Mimi and her three children were riding in the car. The children wanted her to tell them another African story. Suddenly, Mimi remembered the white dress. The story entertained the children until they got home.

Several months passed. One day, as Mimi was gathering things to send to her parents in Africa, eight-year-old Kyndra brought in her new Madame Alexander doll. The beautiful doll had been a gift from her other grandmother. Kyndra handed the doll to her mother with tears streaming down her cheeks. "Here," she said. "Pack this up for Grandma in Africa." Mimi said in disbelief, "But this is your best doll." Kyndra replied without hesitation, "You said that God was worthy of my best."

The package to Africa took one year to arrive by boat. Mimi's mother knew the doll was coming, and she was watching for just the right little girl to receive it. Shortly after Mimi's mother received the package, a newly arrived missionary family came to visit her. One piece of their luggage had been stolen, the suitcase that held all of their young daughter's toys. The next morning, the elegant doll sat in the high chair, waiting for this child, waiting to belong again.

Each of us is involved in the cycle of life. We teach our children the joy of giving, and someday they will teach their children. We are recipients as these truths are passed on. May we give our best simply because God is worthy of our best.

Table Talk:
Look up Zaire on the map. What peoples live in the jungles of Zaire?
How are jungle trees different from ones we have in our yard?
The package took one year to arrive. What were you doing one year ago?
What is the best you have to give?
Who are the poor living near us and how can we give to them?

▾ Epilogue ▾

"Dinner can still be the daily gathering point for the family, the time when many kinds of sustenance are offered. Although the national trend seems to be away from the family table, the healthy families we studied are making a determined effort to offset that trend," said Dolores Curran in *Traits of a Healthy Family*.[1]

It's time to turn the tables on the family trend to spend dinner as a catch-it-when-you-can affair. Many families will have to make sacrifices in order to spend a mealtime together three or four times a week. They may have to reschedule—or drop—lessons, classes, or the habit of staying late at work. That's not easy, and we can't make those sacrifices for you. At best we can try to make your mealtime a bit easier, and we can assure you it's worth the effort.

This book was written with a heart for single parents and the special difficulties they face around mealtime. One evening in our home Alex was out of town and the boys and I sat down to dinner. We were eating Wild Rice Chicken, a recipe that includes water chestnuts. One of the boys discovered that the water chestnuts resembled miniature Frisbees. Enchanted, they began tossing them around the room. I asked them to stop, then pleaded, then hollered—all to no avail. In panic I thought, *What would it be like if I had them to myself every night?*

If you do have children to yourself every night, we're rooting for you. Keep trying new methods and be persistent in your attempt to establish the stability of a dinner, or breakfast, or whatever meal routine.

For all of us, some nights are marred by sibling quarrels. Some nights the meal isn't finished in time. But some nights are magic, well worth the attempt to be consistent and to keep trying. These are the fruits of consistency in keeping a family mealtime.

Remember the young woman who learned, at the table, to recite the presidents when she was in kindergarten? Today she and her grown siblings look forward to any occasion that brings the family together. As they reminisce over the storehouse of dreams and pranks and family learning they experienced at their table, they bring the perspectives they've gained from maturity. They now share how they felt about situations, why they acted as they did.

Children who grow up contributing to the production of a regular meal are better able to maneuver in the kitchen.

If their family table has been enriched by guests, children grow up able to converse with people of all ages and occupations and more sensitive to others' needs. They are more confident stating their opinions.

In November 1993, Oprah Winfrey on her television talk show challenged five families to eat dinner together three to four times a week for a month. Afterward the families appeared on the show with Dr. Steve Wolin, a psychiatrist at the Family Research Center at George Washington University, who has done research pointing to the importance of the ritual of the family dinner hour. It was a tough assignment. One family flatly flunked. Another family ate with the mom present from her hotel room via a conference call. But in general the families liked it. They got to know each other. And they had fun.

Take Oprah's challenge, or take ours. Carve out time at least three or four times a week that works best for your family. Keep the meal simple, keep the tone positive, and keep the benefits for the years to come.

▾ Notes ▾

CHAPTER 1

1. Judith Martin, "Why Family Dinners Are Important," *Rocky Mountain News* (July 4, 1993).
2. Letty Cottin Pogrebin, "Table Talk," *Family Circle* (June 8, 1993): 68.
3. Dolores Curran, *Traits of a Healthy Family* (Minneapolis: Winston Press, Inc., 1983): 31.
4. Ibid., p. 200.

CHAPTER 2

1. Proverbs 14:1 NAS
2. Pogrebin, "Table Talk," 71.
3. Harriet Webster, "Most Important Hour in a Child's Day," *Reader's Digest* 143:856 (Aug. 1993): 86.

CHAPTER 3

1. Alan Bash, "Understanding Different Types of Students," *USA Today* (Sept. 30, 1993): 1D, 6D..
2. Curran, *Traits of a Healthy Family*, 48.
3. Bruce Wilkinson, "Effective Family Devotions, part 1," interview by Dr. James Dobson, Focus on the Family radio broadcast, re-aired Apr. 21-22, 1994.
4. Matthew 16:6; 1 Corinthians 5:6, 7
5. 1 John 4:4b NAS
6. John 15:13 NAS
7. Colossians 4:6 NAS
8. Matthew 5:13 NAS
9. Genesis 19:26 NAS
10. Preston Bruce, "Those Who Serve," *Life* 15:11 (Oct. 30, 1992): 74, 75.
11. Deborah Beroset Diamond, "All Stressed Out," *Ladies' Home Journal* 108 (Nov. 1991): 68.

CHAPTER 4

1. Helen Dollaghan, "Women's Perennial Burden Lightened by Time-Saving Menus," *Denver Post*

(Wed., Mar. 3, 1993): 1E.

2. Kim Newlen, interviewed by Louis Mahoney, "Divine Dinners," *Richmond Times-Dispatch* (Wed., Sept. 22, 1993): F2.

3. Rhonda Barfield, *Eat Well for $50 a Week* (Saint Charles, Mo.: Lilac Publishing, 1993): 11. Available by sending $9.95 + 1.50 postage and handling to Lilac Publishing, Dept. F, P.O. Box 665, St. Charles, MO 63302-0665.

CHAPTER 5

1. Bonnie Runyan McCullough and Susan Walker Monson, *401 Ways to Get Your Kids to Work at Home* (New York: St. Martin's Press, 1981): ix

2. Susan Ginsberg, Ed.D., "Getting Children to Pitch In," *Good Housekeeping* 207 (Sept. 1988): 69.

3. Twila Paris, Preface to "The Joy of the Lord," Sanctuary (Nashville: Star Song, 1991.)

CHAPTER 6

1. Susan Brenna, "Family Traditions: The Power of Knowing Who You Are," *McCall's* 117 (Apr. 1990): 76.

2. Curran, *Traits of a Healthy Family*, 199.

3. Daniel Goleman, "Family Rituals May Promote Better Emotional Adjustment," *The New York Times Health* (Wed., Mar. 11, 1992).

4. Curran, *Traits of a Healthy Family*, 199.

CHAPTER 7

1. 1 Peter 4:9 NAS

2. Genesis 18; 1 Kings 17:8-16.

3. Rachael Crabb with Raeann Hart, *The Personal Touch* (Colorado Springs: NavPress, 1990):

CHAPTER 8

1. Source: International Students, Inc.

2. International Students, Inc., *An American Friend Handbook* (Colorado Springs: International Students, Inc., 1992): 3.

3. Lawson Lau, *The World at Your Doorstep* (Downer's Grove: InterVarsity Press, 1984): 13 from Mark Hanna, "The Great Blind Spot in Missions Today," World Missions Conference at Park Street Church, Boston, Mass., 1975.

4. International Students, Inc., *International Friends* 4:3 (Summer 1993): 3.
5. Mark D. Renta, "Diplomats in Our Backyard," *Newsweek* (Feb. 16, 1987): 10.
6. Ibid.
7. Ibid.
8. ISI, *An American Friend Handbook,* 9.
9. International Students, Inc., *Doorways* 18:4 (July/Aug. 1992): 4.
10. Proverbs 10:12 NAS

CHAPTER 9

1. Linda Burton, Janet Dittmer, and Cheri Loveless, *What's a Smart Woman Like You Doing At Home?* (Washington, D.C.: Acropolis Books, Ltd., 1986): 65, 66.
2. Curran, *Traits of a Healthy Family*, 42.
3. Hermine Hartley, *The Family Book of Manners* (Uhrichsville, Ohio: Barbour and Company, Inc., 1990).
4. Mark 9:36-41 NAS
5. Bob Skold, Jr., *Homefront, Newsletter of the Executive Network,* Denver, (Nov. 1992): 1.
6. Psalm 133:1 NAS

CHAPTER 10

1. Charlene Price, "Fast Food Chains Penetrate New Markets," *USDA Food Review* 16:1 (Jan.-Apr. 1993): 8.
2. Noel Bliscard and James Blaylock, "Slow Growth in Food Spending Expected," *USDA Food Review* 16:2 (May-Aug. 1993):

EPILOGUE

1. Curran, *Traits of a Healthy Family,* 58.

TABLE TOPICS

1. Jim Trelease, *The New Read-Aloud Handbook* (New York: Penguin Books, 1989).
2. Curran, *Traits of a Healthy Family,* 50, 51.
3. The Ungame, all ages version (Anaheim, Calif.: Talicor Inc., 1989).

▾ Index ▾

▾ Notes ▾

▾ Notes ▾

▾ Notes ▾

▾ Notes ▾

▾ Notes ▾

▾ Notes ▾

▾ Notes ▾

▾ Notes ▾

▾ Notes ▾

▾ Notes ▾

Table Talk

Now that you have strengthened your family with the creative suggestions, helpful hints and plenty of delicious new recipes, share this valuable resource with friends, neighbors and family. It's a great gift idea for any time you want to let someone know you care about them and their family.

$9.99 spiral bound
Available at your favorite Christian bookstore.

▾ Focus on the Family Publications ▾

Focus on the Family
This complimentary magazine provides inspiring stories, thought-provoking articles and helpful information for families interested in traditional, biblical values. Each issue also includes a "Focus on the Family" radio broadcast schedule.

Parental Guidance
Close-ups and commentaries on the latest music, movies, television and advertisements directed toward young people. Parents, as well as youthleaders, teachers and pastors will benefit from this indispensable newsletter.

All magazines are published monthly except where otherwise noted. For more information regarding these and other resources, please call Focus on the Family at (719) 531-5181, or write to us at Focus on the Family, Colorado Springs, CO 80995.